DEVELOPMENT RETOLD

Voices from the Field

About the editor:

Gouri Salvi—born 4 March, 1954. She is a freelance journalist with a special interest in gender and development issues. She has worked for over 20 years with magazines—including "Onlooker" in Mumbai and "Sunday" in Calcutta—and with the Women's Feature Service as one of its editors in New Delhi. A book, "Beijing" on the UN's Fourth World Conference on Women, which she helped compile for the Women's Feature Service, was published earlier this year. Besides contributing regularly to various publications, she is currently part of a team involved in research on the forms of censorship that impact women's creative writing in the sub-continent.

DEVELOPMENT RETOLD

Voices from the Field

by
Gouri Salvi

CONCEPT PUBLISHING COMPANY, NEW DELHI-110059

This study was initiated by the Indian Cooperative Union. It was supported and aided by the Association of Voluntary Agencies for Rural Development (AVARD) and HIVOS—India Regional Office, Bangalore. All royalties from the sale of this book are to accrue to the Indian Cooperative Union which is a non-profit organisation.

ISBN 81-7022-798-4 (H.B.)

First Published 1999

Published and Printed by
Ashok Kumar Mittal
Concept Publishing Company
A/15-16, Commercial Block, Mohan Garden
New Delhi-110059 (India)

Phones: 5648039, 5649024
Fax: 091-(11)-5648053

INTRODUCTION

The Golden Jubilee year of India's freedom has come and gone. And even as India's development progresses, haunting questions persist: Whose development? What is the character of development? Does it serve those who are the most needy and neglected? Does it develop their dignity and self-confidence along with improvement in their material conditions? Or does it make them avoidably dependent? Does it deliver that which is promised and on whose behest astronomical sums are spent? These questions must cause us discomfort considering that disparities, unemployment and poverty continue to afflict an intolerable proportion of our population even after five decades of freedom and substantial development effort.

We do seem to get stirred from time to time to reshape development *policy* and related programmes to obtain results. But development *practice* seldom commands our attention. The quality of practice itself depends on the institutional arrangements as well as the background of field workers. Of late, changes in institutional arrangements have figured on the national agenda : State versus market; centralisation versus decentralisation. But there is, as yet, insufficient recognition of the difference that can be made to the character and quality of development by individual field workers—their social awareness and commitment to equity.

This book focusses on selected individuals, with diverse backgrounds, who were drawn into the development field by the dawn of Independence in 1947. The story told here relies on oral history as recalled by these individuals based on their real-life experience—what they did, what they felt and their retrospective reflections on what was right, what was wrong, given the advantage of hindsight.

All of the selected individuals in this study worked with the Indian Cooperative Union (ICU)—a voluntary constructive work organisation, founded soon after Independence at the initiative of Kamaladevi Chattopadhyaya—a vibrant fighter for freedom, social emancipation and the country's cultural assertion.

The exercise brings out that for translation of social ideals and ideas, the individuals at the operational level have to have a measure of social awareness and have to be open to finding out what exactly the specific community being served, wants and regards as "progress", what it expects, what contribution it can itself make towards the attainment of its own preferred goals. That, in turn, ensurs that the individuals in the community gain not only materially but also in self-confidence and dignity. Further, that even if the individuals at the operational level are inexperienced to start with, they can learn given some humility.

The men and women who were drawn to the Indian Cooperative Union came not just in ones or twos but in large numbers. What impelled them ? Their own voices tell the story. In most cases, there was the influence of the freedom movement which explained their social awareness and commitment but, of course, with strong ideological, albeit differing, biases. Invariably, they were individuals who had little prior experience in the kind of activities into which they plunged—whether organising agricultural workers cooperatives, rural credit, or craft persons or setting up industrial enterprises, marketing or export, consumer cooperative stores, labour cooperatives, house building for refugees or running health and educational services.

They learnt much of what they did in the field that was outside the classroom as it were. And much of it they learnt from the people they were serving—whether poor or unemployed. This book draws on the varied and rich experience of a number of individuals who constituted the core of ICU's field workers and helped to generate the process and enabling environment of progress. A message of this study is that the make-up of the individual organisers does make a significant difference to the content and direction of development.

Gouri Salvi did most of the individual interviews. Some interviews were carried out by Ritu Gurha and Jyotsna Bhatnagar on a voluntary basis. Initially, the interviewers had difficulty in getting the individuals to speak about themselves for they had seldom focussed on themselves, or to air critical references to their past experience and associates. Gouri Salvi's persistence, however, persuaded them to talk, to recall the past—some 30 to 50 years ago, and to let go. As a result, the book is enriched and, I believe, it is instructive and relevant to the present-day pattern and pursuit of our development endeavour.

New Delhi
January, 1999

L. C. JAIN

AN OVERVIEW

Post-Independence India. It was a turbulent period for a country trying to find its feet after the horror of Partition and striving to ease the suffering of millions of refugees who arrived at its doorstep seeking shelter and succour. It was also a time of intense debate and dialogue among the newly free, as they tried to arrive at what was best for a fledgling nation in terms of governance, of political system, of social processes. But most of all, it was a time of magical excitement, as almost every Indian felt a sense of deep obligation to consolidate the hard-won freedom and rebuild the nation in tune with the ideals of the freedom movement.

The immediate and most colossal task at hand, of course, was the rehabilitation of refugees. Relief camps in Delhi reeled under a myriad pressures in trying to cope with the mental, physical and emotional traumas that these displaced people had suffered. While administrators and volunteers alike got submerged in the day-to-day fire-fighting to keep the camps running smoothly, it stirred one woman with a wide vision to ask the critical question: "What does the future of these refugees entail?" This question posed by activist and socialist leader, Kamaladevi Chattopadhyaya, after a visit to the relief camp looked after by a Congress volunteer, Lakshmi Chand Jain, set in motion a fascinating process. It was a process that culminated in the birth of an organisation—the Indian Cooperative Union (ICU) which was to leave an indelible mark on that period of the nation's history.

Under Kamaladevi's dynamic leadership a group of committed youngsters came together, fired with the heady dream of rebuilding the nation. They hurled themselves straight into the struggles of the "second revolution"—a social and economic transformation of India. In the context of the refugee situation, Kamaladevi realised that the quickest and most satisfying method of rehabilitation would be self-help. She zeroed in on the idea of a cooperative and set up ICU in record time, "to help the refugees help themselves" in building their lives amid a new (and not always conducive) environment.

It was interesting that when Kamaladevi took the concept of ICU to Gandhiji, seeking his blessings for the venture, he gave his support on condition that he would withdraw it the moment ICU's work became dependent on the government. Evidently, he had anticipated the problems that lay ahead due to tendency of increasing servility to the State. Thus fortified by Gandhiji's blessings, albeit mixed, because of the firm warning, and under Kamaladevi's unwavering guidance, ICU always helped the government in various worthwhile endeavours, yet never gave in to any of its unprincipled policies or its political pressures. Rather than do this, the organisation often preferred to withdraw from its collaboration with the government. Over time and almost as a pattern, therefore, ICU opted out of projects when the government pressure became too stifling and its interference too unbearable.

ICU started off as a "doer" organisation, putting on the mantle of "advocator" much later when it sensed that the official policies stood in the way of building a new "people's India". It soon became a pioneer in many fields—an innovative, gutsy pioneer.

In 1948, for instance, the first project that ICU took up was the resettlement of refugee families on evacuee land outside Delhi. As it happened, there were hundreds of landless agricultural workers in the relief camps of Delhi who yearned for land to cultivate. ICU proposed that these workers be settled on the land left behind by farmers who had migrated to Pakistan. When they tried to get permission for this, they were dismayed to find that the government had already allotted all the evacuee land to various big landlords (many of them government officials) who had migrated from Punjab and Sindh!

Once more it was an outraged Kamaladevi who bluntly asked the leaders of independent India: "How can you profess socialism in one breath and recreate the *zamindari* system in the other ?" Her query, unfortunately, went unanswered but ICU became the first organisation to exhaustively question the social dimensions of the government's rehabilitation policy. When the government continued to drag its feet, the organisation had but one option left. In a revolutionary move, it encouraged and supported the landless refugees to occupy the evacuee farmlands outside Delhi. Many workers of ICU also moved with the refugees to Chhattarpur and other farms to help them organise their work and lives through agricultural cooperatives, and to get together the resources needed for this. Then ICU asked the Prime Minister, Jawaharlal Nehru, to visit Chhattarpur.

After his visit to the farmlands, Nehru, in a letter to the then Home Minister, Sardar Vallabhbhai Patel, observed: "For government officials here to be given evacuee land seems to me improper ... and for very large areas to be given to a single individual also appears to me to be wrong in principle. Someone told me that this was done by some kind of exchange for land in Pakistan. This does not seem to be a sufficient justification. When land is so scarce and so many unfortunate people need it, it seems to me very unfair for large slices to be given to our officials...."

Sardar Patel who was taken by surprise at this bit of information set the wheels in motion immediately and several land allotments to officials were quickly cancelled. ICU had won a significant victory. It was to be one of the many that followed.

Again in 1949, when the government proposed to call in contractors to build the Faridabad township intended for resettlement of displaced persons from the North West Frontier Provinces, ICU brought pressure to bear and got the decision reversed. The organisation convinced the government that the work should, instead, be entrusted to the refugees themselves who would build their own houses through a cooperative endeavour. Consequently, not only did Faridabad come up rapidly and economically, but thousands of refugees learnt new vocations which sustained them for years.

ICU swiftly evolved to become much more than a relief organisation. It took its cue from existing situations and responded creatively to the needs of the time. It opened its arms to an amazing variety of activities but at all times with its feet firmly anchored in the cooperative principles. In 1950, in a letter to Nehru, Kamaladevi very succinctly underscored this unique quality: "The Indian Cooperative Union is not a refugee rehabilitation organisation but essentially a social body that has brought together a band of workers, honorary and otherwise, with faith in the cooperative way of life and is striving not just to provide economic props to the community but more to forge new human relationships between man and man, and man and his vocation, through the cooperative technique."

It was this ability of being sensitive to the people's needs that took ICU on an exciting and vibrant activity-filled journey. It went on to other programmes like rural community development and the development and promotion of handicrafts (through managing the burgeoning Central Cottage Industries Emporium). It also carried out extensive social welfare activities in both rural and urban areas. In addition to this, much later, when the need arose for a cooperative store that could supply items at fair and controlled prices, ICU conceptualised and then successfully launched and ran Delhi's Super Bazar.

Underlying all these activities was the group's constant self-analysis in an ongoing attempt to reconcile practice with ideology. This is where the research section of ICU came in, serving as its agency for self-examination, evaluating projects in hand, collecting data for the formulation of new policies and carrying out surveys for future projects.

Despite these multifarious activities, ICU did hardly any long-term planning. It grew at a pace and in the direction demanded by the ever-changing situation in the country. And over time through trial and error, invaluable lessons were learnt.

ICU realised, for instance, that "cooperation fails if it is reduced to a set of rigid and predetermined rules and procedures; if it does not have the capacity to respect and to adapt itself to the special circumstances and the special ethos of every community". It learnt the importance for all NGOs and other development agencies to respond to the need of the community and then grow from there. The members of ICU also learnt to be intensely aware that they should not fall into the trap of becoming unwieldy and bureaucratic because when this happens, sooner or later, all sense of direction is lost, "principles give place to expediency and idealism succumbs to administrative formalism and commercial logic".

And perhaps, one of the harshest lessons the group learnt was that they have to live with the reality of government and, therefore, they must learn to deal with it at every step.

But no matter how lofty the ideals of any voluntary organisation, or how inspiring its agenda, nothing can be achieved without the right people to transform it into an effective, cohesive agency for progress. More than four decades ago (and after only five years in the field), ICU observed during an exercise in self-inspection:

"We have learnt how exasperating it is in practice to organise and develop cooperatives in the teeth of the opposition of vested interests and the inherited habits and prejudices of the people; and, therefore, how important it is that the organisers and workers of the Union should be persons of sterling qualities, men and women who combine in them the indomitable faith of missionaries and the hard-boiled realism of businessmen; a deep intellectual understanding of the principles and practice of cooperation as well as a deep psychological understanding of human nature; a great self-mastery as well as a great mastery of the difficult art of human relations."

ICU was fortunate to get together just such a band of devoted workers with qualities of staunch integrity and passionate beliefs, who gained and grew in knowledge and experience along with the organisation. They learnt their lessons not from any text-books but, as many of them recall, on the job, in the course of actual struggles in the field. These women and men came from diverse backgrounds: academics, students, activists, journalists, researchers, refugees, farmers. And they brought with them their distinctive and dynamic minds and unique skills which added very special dimensions to the work they undertook at ICU. They were powerful and individualistic personalities, but they shared certain common factors: all of them had been—directly or indirectly—involved with the freedom struggle. And, therefore, each of them brought to his or her work a zeal and dedication that was enviable.

The credit for this must, unquestionably, go to Kamaladevi Chattopadhyaya who attracted these young women and men and then inspired them with the same fervour that she possessed, to make the world a better, more just, more humane place. For her, ICU was a social dream which would awaken the women and men of independent India to their magnificent future through rural development, the revival of handicrafts and the pursuit of civil liberties. She struggled ceaselessly to make this dream a reality—just as she had earlier struggled to end discrimination against women and then to achieve India's freedom. She was a strong, determined individual who, in the cause of justice, had defied first the British and then our own government through the years from Nehru till the days of the Emergency.

L.C. Jain who worked closely with her over many decades once wrote of Kamaladevi: "She was a magnet who drew hundreds of men and women, young and old, to every social movement or cause she stirred or stepped into. All she did was to share the concern and measure the response. For those who showed superficial interest, the encounter was brief, sometimes chilling—she had no patience with passive observers of the scene. But in those who showed even a little spark, she lit a fire: she was all inspiration, light and rock-like support when the occasion demanded.

"She was not an important person, in the commonly understood sense of the adjective. She had no patronage to distribute, she did not attract any sycophants. People flocked to her; but around her they were always a crowd of comrades in a common endeavour."

Kamaladevi passed away in 1988 at the age of 85. But throughout her lifetime, she inspired and influenced hundreds of people in the pursuit of a truly democratic, people-led development which, she believed, would create and sustain the glorious India she and her colleagues envisioned.

This unusual team she pulled together, which she once referred to as people "fired with fresh idealism and moral courage", came to be recognised as the "ICU presence" in those days. It was much like a huge extended family, where each member had created a special place for herself or himself, and where there was always a feeling of warmth and support for each other.

"The selflessness of the group of people in ICU was something different, something exceptional," recalls Swaran Datta, who was actively involved in ICU's social welfare and refugee handicrafts programmes. "That kind of dedication and commitment is difficult to find now. To the extent that Kamaladevi was also concerned about the health of persons working with ICU. This kind of attachment and consideration you don't find now and that is why we were all so motivated to work so hard . . . . If there are such selfless, dedicated people who can inspire you and can bring out your best abilities, even at my age (68 years) today, I would work for them."

Recollections of working with ICU are "a bit like the description of the elephant—it depends on which part of it you touched". Each person on the ICU team "touched" a different part of the organisation at different times, and in turn each was strongly influenced by the years spent with the organisation. Each one, therefore, has a wealth of experiences, information and perceptions to offer, particularly in the context of the aspirations of a voluntary organisation and the kinds of pitfalls that it often confronts. The individual who speak out here have significant insights not only about ICU's workings—its successes as well as its failures—but also about the socio-political realities of some of the most formative years in the nation's life.

"There was something about the time. India was really open, interesting, it had no chips on its shoulder at all. It was self-confident. The self-confidence among Indians and the perceptions of Indians among Indians was that we were free, strong people," recalls Devaki Jain, who worked for a while in ICU's research department. "Today, I think we perceive ourselves as easily bought or sold. We are also petty now; we were not petty then . . . . I think ICU was partly a creature of the period and it was partly unique because it was reconstructing India and it was teaching people from Nehru downwards that you can reconstruct with the people."

The "cooperative" nature of the internal teamwork was what made ICU a true organisation, not just a collection of interesting people. It helped that none of the people were recruited; they recruited themselves to be of use in some way or the other, in the cause of development. In other words, there were no "jobs" being offered at ICU; there was simply a lot of work to be done. And in this convergence for the common goal, the ICU team found a mutual respect for one another where, for the larger social cause, the "self" in each one was, time and again, sub-merged.

"I grew with the job. You see, as the Emporium grew bigger and bigger, so did one's vision expand," remembers Teji Vir Singh, who worked for many years with the Cottage. "Over the years, I came to know the areas of handicrafts in our country inside out. Working closely with the craftspersons, I realised how their entire families used to contribute in creating every one of the items."

Thinking back to that special "ICU spirit" Una Hiremath, who joined the textile department of the Cottage, says: "ICU sent me as an observer member with its buying team all over the centres where fabric was produced. I came back feeling so close not just to the fabric but also to the origins, because once you've seen the weavers, the kind of places they live and work in, your involvement is quite different. That, in a way, set the spirit in which the Cottage and ICU worked. They weren't asking for credentials of your work experience and what degree you held in this line—it was your interest, your attitude that mattered. You got so personally involved that the one thing you forgot to ask was how much would they pay! The commitment that came with this work stayed with you in all you did and that's how textiles and weavers became a life-long interest for me."

Suman Benegal too speaks of this facet of the organisation in her recollections. "The commitment of the first batch that we had was tremendous to the field of handicraft because this was something that was just taking shape and growing . . . . Today when people look at the Cottage, it's all already there," she says. "ICU was the organisation that laid the basis for other cooperatives. If it were not for them, and the kind of people working with them, the Cottage would not have started the way it did. It is because of this solid foundation that even today, although there are many other places, people still look to the Cottage for handicrafts."

This total involvement with the work undertaken, with no thought to any kind of personal gain, is what most of ICU's people remember. And with this involvement came a very special pride in the achievements—perhaps most visible with the Central Cottage Industries Emporium which became a showcase for ICU, as it were.

Says Uma Anand who worked for many years in the purchasing department of handicrafts at the Cottage: "One of the most rewarding experiences was when the craftspersons got national awards for the items that we helped them with . . . and a lot of them did. It was so satisfying to see that through the efforts and help of the Cottage, the standard of living of many of the craftspersons improved and this was one of the basic ICU aims."

This sense of achievement at a job well done is all too evident in Fori Nehru's voice too, when she remembers how, over time, the Cottage Emporium became a byword in the whole country. "Had the Emporium kept a visitors' book it would have been a Who's Who not just of India but of the whole world," she says. "It became like the Taj Mahal—you had to see it. Except that from Delhi the

Taj was far away but the Emporium was on Janpath! It was a throbbing institution and a glory to everyone involved in it."

Anyone who worked with the organisation was most impacted by the ideals it cherished. "The role played by ICU in those times, either individually or organisationally in different fields, was tremendous," remarks Bharat Sahai, the Administrative Secretary. "There was a large number of boys and girls who came in touch with us and became very influenced by the ICU philosophy.... Working together with others at ICU made me a more disciplined person. The training had an impact on me to do things correctly, to do them in time and to not become biased."

This "ICU philosophy" that he hints at is perhaps revealed most lucidly by the organisation's General Secretary, L.C. Jain, when he explains: "Working with the farmers' cooperatives became a critical education for us—we learnt that our excitement about cooperatives, about its democracy and its concept was fine but when we applied it to a particular field like farming, then exactly to what extent the individual farmers would cooperate with one another and for what purpose, or what they would do individually, all this could not be a matter of ideology; it must be a matter of practical wisdom of the people who were involved and of their ability to do it. Because we were not actually doing the work; we were only prescribing it for them. ICU, therefore, evolved very rapidly out of an ideological bind. Otherwise there would have been the danger that instead of helping them with rehabilitation, we would have tried to struggle with them. We might have insisted that they should lead the pattern of life that we thought was proper for them. This is where Kamaladevi's combination of research, independent study and survey of whatever we were undertaking was useful. So much so that it became an armoury for carrying out any action programme and getting a feedback on it.

"The other important thing we had to remember was that no matter how good we were, we were only peripheral to the people we were working with. It was essentially their life; they were rebuilding it. I think as NGOs go, ICU was a model in that sense—in administration, accounts, maintenance, team spirit. In this, Kamaladevi's ground rules and principles were fundamental in helping us move forward . . . . So with the farmers, the refugees and the other groups that we dealt with, we were acutely aware that we were not the mothers; we were the midwives. The baby was theirs. We were there to ease the pain and that was it. That was our role. Which meant respecting their ability to mind their own business without us; that we were there to promote self-help—this was fundamental to ICU's policy."

But of course, as there were successes, there were also failures. "ICU as a voluntary non-profit organisation made path-breaking and innovative forays into economic and social development—a paradigm for others to follow. But nothing fails like success in India (and perhaps elsewhere too)," Som Benegal, ICU's Publicity Manager, recalls. "Venal, rapacious, self-seekers interested only in their narrow interests have wiped out all the sterling achievements of ICU and reduced not only the organisation but the whole cooperative movement to a shadow, a grotesque caricature of its one-time grandeur. But that is the irony and tragedy of change. And yet the spirit, which ICU engendered, lives on, at least among those who carried it to its peak."

In a somewhat similar vein, Sitaram Goel, who made invaluable contributions to ICU's extensive research, notes: "ICU did great work because behind it there was no careerism. The people there really wanted to do something. And although the cooperative experiments in Faridabad failed, the rehabilitation of the refugees was simply great work done by ICU, like which there is no other example...Organisations like ICU, I think, just cannot work . . . . We should not forget that whatever success was achieved by ICU was more due to the type of people who supported it . . . ."

Some of the others too agree with this perception. For instance, Dharampal says: "Basically, ICU was a spontaneous effort to solve some pressing problems. Which it did within its capacity, its manpower, the intellectual talents available to it and so on. But ICU didn't become a movement. We may have thought it would become a movement but maybe we didn't think enough of it."

Narendra Nath Datta—first as Camp Commandant at Faridabad, and then as the first General Manager of the Super Bazar—saw ICU through its ups and downs. He says today, with some distress:

"Those were the days of idealism when we thought the cooperative movement and the trade union movement would provide the total solution for the country. Unfortunately, nothing like that happened. The Super Bazar did a great job and other similar stores sprung up elsewhere in the country too. Initially, the Super Bazar was a totally cooperative venture. But later on it got into the rut of a government department. Members were enrolled, no meetings were called; government began to nominate the board of management. And then came the tussle of the politicians—who should become the chairman, etc. I saw the changes in the Super Bazar even while I was there. The politicians had taken over and made a complete mess of it. The objective with which it had been set up—that it should be a cooperative institution in which members will have a say in all that happens—nothing of that sort happened . . . ."

Amba Prasad, who handled the crucial market intelligence and members' relations for the Super Bazar, goes even a step further to debate the very concept of cooperatives. "I feel today that cooperatives are completely out of tune in the country. Now you don't expect anything from them. Under globalisation and privatisation schemes, cooperatives have lost their relevance," he says. "But having said all this, I still feel that if you want real people's participation, there is no other institution except cooperatives which can bring people together.... Most of the big names of earlier cooperatives are frustrated today and the reason is the complete politicisation of cooperatives.... cooperatives are no more the tools of development and social justice."

Carrying forward the argument against the politicisation of and government interference in cooperatives, B.L. Dhar says, "ICU caused a considerable change in my attitude towards the cooperative movement. Earlier, I was trained to think that without active government assistance and supervision there can be no cooperative movement ... (but) I realised that if people organise themselves voluntarily, they can do things better without much government help and supervision. In India there has always been a feeling that we should go to the government, that it is a *maibaap* for whatever one wants. ICU demonstrated that people could stand on their own and succeed in achieving their goals.

"The most important lesson learnt from ICU is that cooperatives have to be independent. The only cooperative which will succeed, in my opinion, is the one that has full support and patronage of its members and will help its members in achieving something tangible. ... it will succeed only when it has the loyalty of its members. Anything which is totally controlled by the government will not succeed. One of the biggest problems in India is that cooperatives are totally controlled by the government and very few decisions can be made by the cooperatives themselves. The first thing that needs to be done is to free the cooperatives from the clutches of the government. The law must change and cooperatives should have independence."

ICU's Rural Development Secretary, Gopi Krishan's views converge almost entirely with this. "Bureaucratic red tape and loopholes in the government laws make it very difficult for cooperatives to become viable enterprises," he points out. "Despite some successful examples, most have failed to take off because the cooperative rules of State governments are very complicated. The movement cannot succeed unless cooperatives are made totally public enterprises."

So then, should ICU somehow have struck roots and survived? One of the many answers to this much-debated question is provided by Devaki Jain who says: "I do know that Kamaladevi, Lakshmi and Gopiji always had this ideology—which in a sense is partly Gandhian and partly the ideology of real freedom fighters—that no institution is worth its name if it has to be led by the same people. Any institution which persists in doing a job forever shows that the job is not well done. I think institutions like ICU should exist only if they're idealistic and visionary. I think institutions like ICU were born only to show that people had the strength to build their own lives. Many people feel that if ICU had been more realistic it would have survived. Why should it survive? When survival becomes a basic principle, then those visions go. I'm very clear in my mind that it is only vision and that totally revolutionary role that makes an NGO...."

And so the debates go on. In the pages that follow what emerges is an abundance of rich memories—memories replete with happiness, with the satisfaction of having contributed meaningfully in whatever measure. However, at times, there is also a sense of bitterness at things not having worked out quite as expected; a sense of loss that an extraordinary venture did not last long enough. But if there is one thing that shines through the oral histories of these people who made ICU what it was, it is a deep and abiding faith in the values, the ideas and the ideals that the organisation stood for with passionate conviction—and the belief that if those values and ideals have outlived ICU in one way or another, then the institution did succeed in performing its mission.

GOURI SALVI

CONTENT

SECTION I

ONE

"We had to remember that no matter how good we were, we were only peripheral to the people with whom we worked. It was essentially their life; they were rebuilding it."

— *L.C. Jain*

Ques: Can you recall your days as a student leader ?

Ans: I had been very active from the 1942 Quit India movement onwards. Up to 1945 we were part of the underground movement. I was the underground messenger for Aruna Asaf Ali, Devdas Gandhi and others. Because my father was the Secretary of the Delhi Pradesh Congress Party for over 15 years, all these leaders relied on known characters—so for underground contacts it was always the son or daughter of one of the political prisoners (my father too was in jail). Many of us, therefore, were together in the underground network and we assumed that we could trust each other. In that network I found my own place for recognition, as it were. Early in 1943, I carried out a special secret mission for Devdas Gandhi—contacting prisoners in Multan jail to apprise them of Gandhi's indefinite fast. In addition as a student leader, I was entrusted with the job of organising a cell of 5 or 6 reliable students in each of the colleges and high schools in Delhi. This network distributed underground literature, organised rapid strikes and contacts with pro-freedom teachers.

By the time the Indian National Army (INA) prisoners' trial took place here in Delhi at the Red Fort (in 1946), we were no longer underground and had already come into some prominence. On the issue of INA, the Congress leadership got divided on whether or not much should be made of Subhash Bose. By that time I was a prominent student leader and some of us as student leaders fought for the INA prisoners. We decided to defy the Congress and hold a demonstration at the Red Fort at the time of the INA trial. Which we did. Then we had a students' convention to which Congress leaders came and made critical speeches about our role. I remember ordering them (Sri Prakasa, Asaf Ali) off the stage saying that this was our convention, they were honoured guests but they could not use our platform to damn us. So there was this whole build-up and I came to occupy a certain place in the political arena.

Around this time the provisional government had been formed with Jawaharlal Nehru as Vice-President. He wanted to hold the Asian Relations Conference here in Delhi, even before India's formal attainment of freedom. Liaquat Ali as Finance Minister vetoed the proposal. So, Nehru asked the Indian Council of World Affairs (ICWA) to organise it. Nehru got Sarojini Naidu to be the chairperson of the Reception Committee for the Conference. She was new to Delhi; Nehru was also new to Delhi, ICWA was in its infancy—a tiny set-up. It meant that if they were to organise an international conference they would need volunteers. So those of us who were active political student leaders were summoned to join the Asian Relations Conference as organisers. Thus, Raj Krishna, Som Benegal, myself and others, including H.V. Venkatsubbiah, became the Secretariat of the Conference. Nehru summoned us and said: "This is not a Congress *tamasha*; this is an international conference—India's first. It must be of that standard." Sarojini Naidu was our mother, as it were. She was a delight. She gave us total independence and we delivered the conference organisation to a level that Nehru was pleased. He gave us tea at the Imperial Hotel afterwards.

By that time communal rioting had started and a relief committee was set up under Sucheta Kripalani by the AICC. They were looking for volunteers. I don't know who exactly suggested my name, but it was a very small world at that time: you either came via Sarojini Naidu or via Nehru. I was called in late one evening by Sucheta Kripalani to go and take charge right away of the refugee camp at Kingsway where there had been communal violence. The person who was in charge was to be removed by the police that evening and they wanted a political replacement—someone with whom they could be certain that communal violence could be contained. Nehru had been particularly happy with my role in the Asian Relations Conference, so when the camp in-charge had to be removed, my name came up as a replacement. I was an active political student leader at that time, doing M.A. final (History). However, when

Sucheta Kripalani said I had to go immediately, I went to the camp and took charge, and that was the last I saw of the University.

Ques: Can you describe the camp ?

Ans: This was a relief camp, mainly to ensure that the 10,000 refugees there got tents, food, a small health clinic, trench latrines, water, schools and things like that. Tempers were very high because people had just gone through the trauma of Partition. One day, in the middle of all this, Kamaladevi Chattopadhyaya visited the camp. My camp was regarded as a well-organised camp and a lot of visitors used to come—Nehru came, Lady Mountbatten came. I took Kamladevi around the camp. She saw everything and then sat down and asked what was the future of these people ? I said I did not know as I was just submerged in their day-to-day problems. But I did tell her that they had, in fact, been raising this very question, but I didn't have a clue. I told her that a number of them were agricultural workers and what they really wanted was land. As a socialist, Kamaladevi had a very imperious way of asking that question. Not really questioning you but asking the larger question. She was really not demanding an answer from me but was raising the question to find if anyone at all had the answer. That question of hers just gripped me and I felt that I must get out of this feeling that I've done a lot of good work by organising the camp.

After she left I was really disturbed. I realised that this was the main question that we should be addressing. At that time, I was doing just the relief part.

Ques: How did the idea of the Indian Cooperative Union come up ?

Ans: Two days later Kamaladevi phoned me, asking me to come to a meeting she had called. At that meeting there were quite a few socialists. She gave a report of her visit to my camp; brought up the questions she had asked me and the fact that I, like everybody else, had no clue about what was to be done. It was this meeting which decided to set up an organisation which would help these people build a new life. It was Kamaladevi's idea that it must be a cooperative effort.

Kamaladevi had moved fast. A week later, someone brought a typed memorandum of association for setting up the Indian Cooperative Union (ICU) to be filed for registration. I later learnt that there was one Ramalingam Chettiar, MP, a great cooperator from the South, who had helped her with the memorandum. I was asked to be a promoter for ICU. At that time, I did not know what cooperatives were really all about. So I went to Raj Krishna's house at night for advice. He explained what the cooperative implies and convinced me that it was a good idea. Then Kamaladevi started to pursue the registration. But she said that whether the society was registered or not, we must move ahead with rehabilitation of these people. She felt we should start with the landless agricultural workers. She asked me to conduct rapidly what we now call a socio-economic survey: find out who they are; how many households; what is their social and occupational, background, their ideas about the future, etc. The survey didn't take much time because those people themselves were eager to give me all the information, once they knew that we were trying to help in their rehabilitation.

Once that was done, a remarkable development took place. The City Magistrate of Delhi, Mohinder Singh Bedi, came to see me at the refugee camp and told me that he wanted all the landless agricultural workers from the camp to move to the villages. He explained that refugee land in Mehrauli had been allotted to some people including the Deputy Commissioner, but they could not find labour. I told him that, in fact, we were looking for land for these people to work as owners and not as labour. He assured me that there was no more land in Delhi to be found. I asked for a few days' time and reported this to Kamaladevi. She asked the government if some of that land which the Deputy Commissioner and other landlords had taken could be given to these people but was told that all refugee land had already been allotted to refugee landlords. This was the land left behind by Muslim cultivators who had gone to Pakistan and it was all given to big landlords. According to prevailing report, M.S. Randhawa (ICS) had 1,000 acres allotted to him; Sir Datar Singh, advisor to the Ministry of Agriculture, had 2,500 acres allotted; M.S. Sahani, principal of the law college who was a Sindhi refugee, had 600 acres allotted. Kamaladevi felt, then, that the only way out was to occupy this land.

I told the people in the camp if they were game, we were behind them and they should occupy the land, otherwise it was going to take a very long time for anything to work out. They said that they needed staying power for six months, that is till the crop was ready. So I gave them six months of rations from the camp stores. Overnight, we moved about 200 families with rations and they occupied the land.

Kamaladevi asked me to pull out of the refugee camp because now these agricultural workers would need someone to organise things there. By this time a Rehabilitation Commissioner had been appointed and Sucheta Kripalani asked me to talk to him. When I went to him, he emphatically refused to let me go as this was "one of our good camps". He said, but Kamaladevi convinced him that it was very important that I should move to the villages and help to organise these people on the land. From there onwards, it was all action.

Ques: What were some of your more memorable experiences from the relief camp days ?

Ans: Well, there were many experiences but I did have one last sorrow, as it were.

Nehru's visit to my camp had become quite an experience. Till then, he had been abused and pushed around at every refugee camp that he visited. The refugees were in a temper. They used to tell him that if what had happened to their daughters—molestation and rape—happened to his daughter, only then would he understand their suffering. They would blame him for partitioning the country and would say that he had caused their ruin. It was a terrible experience for him.

When Edwina Mountbatten came to my camp, she said to me before she left: "This is the camp that Jawahar should visit." The next day there was a phone call saying that the Prime Minister wanted to visit the camp shortly. And then all the security people descended. I said to the Deputy Commissioner: "If security is coming here, then Nehru is not coming to my camp. The people of the camp are his security." But the Deputy Commissioner would not hear none of it. He said: we have a responsibility. You know how he has been pushed around at these camps. We cannot take any risk." I asked him to give me three days to access whether the camp inmates could guarantee Nehru's security.

I called the camp leaders immediately and informed them that Nehru was likely to visit our camp. Their spontaneous reaction was : *"Aane do usko, bata dengey."* (Let him come, we'll show him!) I explained to them about the Partition and why they could not blame Nehru alone—that there was a whole history behind it. I assured them that we all understood their suffering, but we should try not to make the situation any worse than it already was. I also explained to them about the police security for Nehru's visit and my desire not to have a large security force in our camp. I pleaded that if they assured me that they would organise the camp residents and ensure Nehru's security, only then it was worth inviting him here.

Soon the overwhelming sentiment among the refugees was that they would give their life for Jawaharlal and make sure that not a hair on his head was harmed while he visited the camp. I conveyed to the Deputy Commissioner that we could guarantee Nehru's safety. He sent his intelligence men who confirmed that the atmosphere in the camp was transformed and the refugees were looking forward to the visit and welcoming Nehru. It was agreed that the police would wait outside the camp and the camp leaders would receive Nehru as he alighted from the car, and conduct his visit

Then the leaders and I discussed as to what they would say to him. I suggested that if I was in their place I would simply say : "Panditji, such a huge burden has fallen on your shoulders, is there any way in which we can share that burden?" But they wanted to know what would happen to their demands. I said that he would definitely ask for their demands but that they should not start with demands—just give love; just say that they wanted to lessen his burden. I suggested that they should however write down their demands on a piece of paper and give it to him only if the time was right. They agreed unanimously.

When Nehru came, I introduced him to the camp leaders. At which point an old man, the chairman of the Camp Committee, got up and made an emotional speech in a flowery language ! Nehru had tears in his eyes. He just embraced this man, saying that he understood their grief but that he had never before heard such soothing words. He then asked if there was anything that he could do for them. At that point, the leader took out the list which Panditji read, promising to do whatever he could. As he was leaving, he took me aside and suggested that Gandhiji should come to the camp for "this experience".

I said that would be our privilege. He promised to arrange for Gandhiji's visit. But alas, a few days later, Gandhiji was shot dead. The entire, camp men and women, wept. They didn't sleep, they didn't eat. They walked all the way to Rajghat.

In my whole experience of the relief operations, this remained the saddest moment. It was all the more poignant because my experience of the relief camp had begun with thoughts of Gandhiji. When I was first sent here by Sucheta Kripalani, there was a lot of violence in the camp. The group of people who were upset that I had been sent to replace the earlier camp in-charge, who was a refugee and one of them, began throwing stones at my barrack that very first night. Many colleagues felt that we should call in the police. But at that moment, suddenly Gandhiji came to my mind and I thought to myself, what would he think if he heard that I'd set the police on refugees? I refused. We stuck it out for the night and by the early hours of the morning they had gone. The next day I held a meeting at each barrack and explained to the refugee inmates exactly what had happened that night. I also told them that if they were very unhappy with me, I would leave. The result was that by the end of the evening, a voluntary committee had been set up for each barrack to assist in the camp management.

I was happy that an alternative force to the police had been built. They had a separate meeting and decided to expel all the gangsters. They came to me with this resolution. Again Gandhiji came to my mind, asking if this was the right thing to do. I said to the leaders that though misguided these too were our children and we should not expel them. Word must have got around because the next morning some of these so-called "gangsters" came to me and thanked me. They assured me that they would not cause any trouble and the matter ended there.

So my very first step into that camp had brought Gandhiji as a frame of reference to me. Why he came, how he came, till today I have no clue. But he entered in my mind in a forcible way that was strange for me, who was one of the 1942-*wallahs,* the bomb-*wallahs,* who never believed that freedom would come through non-violence. But now the very thought of him helped me to survive. And all through my stay in the relief camp, I always felt that he was there, standing behind me. So I was more than charged with the thought of Gandhiji coming to the camp following Nehru's visit. Alas, it was not to be.

Ques: Chhattarpur must have been a totally different experience ?

Ans: I became the first cooperative organiser for Chhattarpur village to find out from these people what was it that was needed—like seed, water, bullocks, etc. This was my first training in problems of agriculture at the ground level, seeing what problems arise and what happens. Sardar Bhag Singh was the leader of the Chhattarpur cooperative which was called the Sachkhand Multipurpose Cooperative Society. He was truly a fantastic leader—illiterate, but with tremendous self-confidence. A tall, huge *sardarji*, he was a picture of confidence. He told me that more organisers were needed. Word got around and we started getting more volunteers and it became a team. Kamaladevi was a big draw so young people, who were socialists and wanted to do some constructive work would come to the party office and from there they would be sent to Kamaladevi and she would then send them to Chhattarpur. But not all of them came through the socialist connections. For instance, in the refugee camp there was Gopi Krishan, who is the secretary of ICU. He was with me in the Purana Qila relief camp. He met Kamaladevi and decided to join. He remained as rural secretary through the entire period. He did not have a rural background, but the very idea that we would go to the villages and work just seemed to attract people.

We would have a lot of debates: should we live in the village or outside; what kind of clothes should we wear; what impact would it have. But Kamaladevi cured us of all that and said that we didn't have to live there because our living there might create a sense of dependency. It should be a situation where they come to you only if they need something. In that case, the effort of coming will decide if it is worth it. Secondly, wear simple clothes but don't occupy yourselves too much with that because whether you are naked or clothed, people are sharp enough to recognise who is genuine and who is not and whether you really mean well by them. All this was education for us. In terms of methodology too, she said don't build up dependence. Keep yourself at a distance. Later on she developed the concept that we must not stay in any one place for too long because we would start feeling that without us things would not move—which would denote that we had, in fact, achieved nothing. Our business was to create conditions in which the people can do their business, as she put it. We should not supplant their efforts. These concepts were not written in any book but became our truths.

Ques: What were some of the hurdles you faced at these villages ?

Ans: One of the major problems that I faced at that time had something to do with non-refugee families who were already living on the village land. In the village habitat they had to all live together and the problem of relationships, tensions, accommodation, etc., that came up became quite critical. It was the notions of the Delhiwallahs versus the Punjabis. Many of the Sikh farmers who came as refugees ate meat and in this village eating eggs and meat was not acceptable. So socially and culturally, there were tensions. This issue of harmonious living took us almost a year. The general principles that India was free, that Partition had taken place and refugees would have to be accommodated, were accepted but when it came to living together, these principles got forgotten. I had to keep talking to them to ease tensions. I must say that the older, senior villagers were very considerate—it was their largeness which asserted itself. In the case of the refugees, they were at pains to be accepted. Thus, there was a kind of logic working on both sides which finally smoothened the friction. In the whole process of rehabilitation it became an example. Then there were the problems of gathering the requisite agricultural wherewithal to get them going and getting them familiar with markets for seeds, fertilisers, etc.

At one stage, we succeeded in bringing Nehru to Mehrauli to show him the work that was going on and told him that this land was not allotted to these people but was in the name of Randhawa and others. He was livid. He wrote a letter to Sardar Patel demanding to know how the ICS men had taken all that land. This was when the policy changed, in terms of the allotment of refugee land not going to landlords but going to the cultivators, which made room for many of these people getting accepted. But the wickedness of our system came to the fore. They said allotments would be made in the individual names and not to their cooperative. We explained that these families had formed a cooperative so the allotment should be in the name of the cooperative. Although they said that the policy was to encourage cooperatives, we could not budge the system on this very crucial issue. So land was given to individuals and over the years the farm houses that have come up in the Chhattarpur area came into existence, because the Delhi elite were able to buy off individuals; they would not have been able to buy off the cooperatives.

Later, the government started talking about joint farming ventures with the Congress' Nagpur Resolution. We actually started with joint farming but ours broke up in an evolutionary sense. In the beginning, everything was scarce, so the farmers would use the same ploughs even if they were broken, the same bullocks, etc. Little resources covered big land. As they progressed, we found that the farmers had marked out their individual fields in their own minds. We did case studies and found out that the objective situation had changed and, therefore, they had changed their operations from joint farming to individual farming. So we felt that we should respect it. Why should we impose an ideology on them? If they found that cooperation was required only for "X" and not for "Y" circumstances, why should we insist that they must have it for "Y" too? It became a critical education for us—we learnt that our excitement about cooperatives, about its democracy and its concept was fine but when we applied it to a particular field like farming, then exactly to what extent the individuals would cooperate with one another and for what purpose, or what they would do individually, all this could not be a matter of ideology; it must be a matter of practical wisdom of the people who were involved and of their ability to do it. We were not actually doing the work; we were only prescribing it for them. ICU, therefore, evolved very rapidly out of an ideological bind. Otherwise there would have been the danger that instead of helping them with rehabilitation, we would have tried to struggle with them. We might have insisted that they should lead the pattern of life that we thought was proper for them. This is where Kamaladevi's combination of research, independent study and survey of whatever we were undertaking was useful. So much so that it became an armoury for carrying out any action programme and getting a feedback from the people.

Ques: How long did you carry on at Chhattarpur ?

Ans: At one stage I was pulled out of village Chhattarpur. A crisis was developing in Faridabad where they were not agricultural refugees but they were mainly urban refugees—pathans from the North West Frontier. They had made Nehru' s life miserable. They would camp outside his house. They would sleep during the day and shout slogans at night when Nehru slept. And yet, Nehru and others were committed and they all wanted to treat them well. Mridula Sarabhai, who was very close to Nehru and other leaders like Khan Abdul Ghaffar Khan and Sheikh Abdullah, was working with the recovery of abducted women—Hindu and Muslim women who were abducted during the communal riots. My father was working with her and I too had come to know her. She asked Kamaladevi whether I could come and help in Faridabad. So Mridula, myself and Kamaladevi went to Faridabad and met the refugees. They were very hostile, yet they felt that if Nehru was not able to do anything, nobody else could.

Ques: What were their grievances at that point ?

Ans: They were moneylenders, shopkeepers and they were told that the government was going to build houses for them here. But they wanted to know what they were supposed to do. In those days, nobody knew the answer to this; Nehru would say something will be done. These were millions of refugees and when they demonstrated, the only solution for the administration was the police and *lathi* charge. So those who were aggravated got even more aggravated. We spent some hours there and in the late evening got ready to leave. At that moment I suddenly said that I wanted to stay on with these people because it seemed so odd to leave when they were so charged and wanted to tell us their stories. So I stayed on that night and, as expected, somebody took me into his tent. A lot of people gathered and wanted to know who I was. When I told them about myself and the work I had been doing they seemed interested. So it became a dialogue and slowly a relationship built up—these Frontier pathans have that characteristic: if they embrace you, they embrace you totally. In the morning when I told them I was going they persuaded me to stay on. In any case, I spent the day and then in the evening went and reported to Mridula and Kamaladevi. They went to report to Nehru. Nehru then asked Kamaladevi if ICU would go to Faridabad and help there. At that time, Mridula told Kamaladevi that I had to be allowed to go to Faridabad. So for three years I was at Faridabad.

Then we had a crisis with the government in Faridabad, at which stage ICU withdrew and walked out. (That story is covered in *City of Hope—the Faridabad Story.*) Then I came back to ICU in Delhi.

Ques: How did ICU—and with it, you yourself—evolve over the years ?

Ans: First of all, in my own evolution in public work, that entire period in the relief camp never made me miss the university; I never went back to the classroom.

In the meantime, two major dimensions were being built. One was regarding the scale on which we had to operate and the diversity of activities. And the other was a pronounced sense of "I" which was there partly during the Quit India movement and even later in the refugee camp. My entry into the cooperative movement suddenly opened the third eye to the fact that there were also other people with whom you had to work and that it could only be team work. I then started evolving my role through reduction—that if there is someone who can be doing a particular work, then I shouldn't be doing it. That also left enough space for each other and we were not treading on one another's toes. I must say that not once in my 40 years of association did I come across any confrontation with anyone saying that this is my domain and why are you coming into it. Our purpose was to create conditions in which these people could be rehabilitated, and the important thing was to retain the team, enlarge it and more than that to enable it to function effectively. I had been to no management school; I had no training in this. It was a training taught by life and its compulsions. Somewhere it seems to have entered my bones that this work could not be accomplished unless there was this accommodation constantly.

The other important thing we had to remember was that no matter how good we were, we were only peripheral to the very people with whom we worked. It was essentially their life; they were rebuilding it. I think as NGOs go, ICU was a model in that sense—in administration, accounts, maintenance, team spirit. In this, Kamaladevi's ground rules and principles were fundamental in helping us move forward. Now, she too had no experience, so she herself must have been reacting and evolving. So with the farmers, the refugees and other groups that we dealt with , we were acutely aware that we were not the mothers, we were the midwives. The baby was theirs. We were there to ease the pain and that was it. That was our role. Which meant respecting their ability to mind their own business without us; that we were there to promote self-help—this was fundamental to the cooperative union's philosophy.

We were also acutely aware of what the organisation was set up for. Therefore, the culture of the organisation, its personalities, its bending and accommodating qualities got determined by our awareness that we were a serving platform. Naturally, then, it affected our personalities—we had to have ground rules to take decisions in relation to co-workers, in relation to the community we were serving.

The third dimension that grew simultaneously was our whole experience with the government. As our activities grew, the points of contact and conflict also enlarged. Later, I was moved around quite a bit by Kamaladevi who felt that I should not be so involved in field work but get into writing notes, drafting letters, writing reports and studies, etc. It used to be a pain in the neck for me to write anything! I used to be a good speaker during the freedom movement but writing was a different matter altogether. And this is when my whole turnabout came, with more exposure to the government and with my developing a wickedness to deal with their wickedness—which was a completely different experience than dealing with people. With people, no matter where we worked—and we worked day and night—we were never tired and there was no question of despondency. But if you had to deal with the government then your whole mental outlook and attitude changes because there is a whole set of people you are looking at with less than respect. It was a total antithesis of what we were doing. Earlier, in the face of conflict I used to be conciliatory; then in dealing with the government I got the fighting spirit from Kamaladevi who would say that it's important to protect the work we were doing. With the government the starting point was distrust whereas our starting point always was trust.

Ques: What would you list as some of the major challenges you faced in the actual working of ICU ?

Ans: I can think of three challenges right away. First was when ICU tried to adopt a ceiling on the honorarium for its organisers. The ceiling was fixed at Rs. 500 a month. For almost 20 years, we were able to adhere to it in so far as our main organisers were concerned. But the scheme ran into a challenge when ICU's programme of marketing handicrafts and handlooms expanded through the Central Cottage Industries Emporium and we had to employ persons for specialised work and professional skills. In fixing their salaries, ICU was influenced more by the earnings of the craftsmen. But soon they started to compare their emoluments with those of the shop employees in the Connaught Place area.

ICU was slow to respond but recognised that this was, perhaps, inevitable, and for the first time engaged the services of a management expert to devise pay scales (comparative to the market). Once that was done for a section of the workers, it became difficult to resist the demand that pay scales be applied to all. Imperceptibly, ICU lost its character as a social platform and acquired a new personality of an "employer".

Very soon, the trade union movement took notice, particularly of the Cottage Industries Emporium, and soon staff unions were formed. ICU had a dialogue with the leaders of the trade union movement to evolve an understanding about the nature of relationship between a cooperative and the trade union. But it made no headway. ICU then came up with a proposal to suggest to the trade unions that it was willing to hand over the entire management of the Cottage Industries Exporium to the staff union. Their argument was that if the trade union took over the management, it would become an employer. Against whom, then, would they agitate? This would destroy the fire power of the trade union. The matter ended there in relation to staff unions in ICU. But as expected, politicians jumped into the fray. Rajkumari Amrit Kaur, till then a Union Minister of Health, became President of the staff union! By which time ICU's plans to divest itself of "doing" activities had matured and the largest unit—the Cottage—was handed back to the government which turned it into a Corporation.

Later, at a larger level, ICU pursued this as an issue in principle. It was able to get the support of JP (Jayaprakash Narayan) to convene a meeting of the representatives of all India trade unions and cooperative leaders to discuss whether in the wider socio-economic context of India, the trade unions and the cooperative movement did not have a commonality of interest. It was a successful two-day encounter but, in effect, the understanding did not go very far.

The second big issue was the question mark (if not a charge) which Kamaladevi and I faced from time to time from within and outside ICU, that by running the Cottage Emporium were we not giving an elitist twist to the organisation. We kept explaining that those who made the charge looked only at the customers, and that the rationale for ICU to go into it was its concern for the craftspersons and the artisans across the country who were grossly under-employed and facing a threat to their income and survival in the post-Independence period. Marketing was a link to life for them.

We had also set up a florist counter at the Cottage. The counter was patronised by those who gift flowers, that is, naturally the elite. But the reason ICU had set it up was to help one of the farmers near Chhattarpur where ICU was engaged in rural development work. This farmer was growing flowers and wanted a place where he could have direct access to the customers rather than go through a middleman. Similarly, the handloom weavers in Delhi who often made attractive furnishing fabrics were the first to approach ICU for a direct outlet to consumers. Furnishing fabrics too can be afforded only by the better off. Thus, through catering to consumers—elite or non-elite—ICU's central concern was the under-employed urban/ rural producer.

The third challenge we faced was the pressure to align with one political party or the other. Kamaladevi, I and others had given up active politics because we felt that the work that we had started could be best conducted under non-party political auspices. In fact, the first political gathering ICU assembled was to raise the issue of national policy towards allotment of land to the landless refugee workers as against refugee landlords. Invitations were sent to all political parties and they all responded. But because some of us were from previous socialist party affiliations, our past kept on shadowing us. For example, when the most prestigious firm of chartered accountants of Delhi at that time, Vaidyanath Aiyer Co., were proposed by ICU to be its auditors, a question was raised by some in the Congress Party that Aiyer was a socialist party associate!

Later, when ICU raised doubts about the efficacy of the government policy of cooperative farming initiated by the Congress Party at the Nagpur Session, we were at once dubbed by the Congress and the leftists as anti-Congress, pro-capitalist and pro-American. So much so that Nehru, who used to frequently contribute to ICU for different programmes, declined a request by ICU for a contribution to its endowment fund. His reasoning was that "in the prevailing circumstances of controversy over the issue of cooperative farming" any contribution by him to ICU might be misconstrued.

It is important to make note of all this because in the past 25 years—eversince Indira Gandhi came to head the government—voluntary organisations in general were often subjected to the charge of being under the influence of a "foreign hand". And although a donor like the Ford Foundation was making grants only after government approval, the recipient organisations still remained vulnerable to political attack by the Congress and Communist parties. And yet it was during this period that the government created a nodal agency to receive and disburse foreign funds to voluntary organisations and enacted the FCRA (Foreign Contributions Regulation Act) which requires prior government permission for accepting any foreign donation. But none of it is a protection against uninformed or biased assault. Over the last 50 years, no one has yet found a way in which voluntary organisations can really shield themselves from this kind of sporadic attacks on their integrity in terms of receiving foreign funds for their programmes.

Ques: What was your role during the Kudal Commission days ?

Ans: This happened when the Gandhian organisations rallied together under JP's call to oppose the Emergency in the '70s. Opposition to the Emergency was not regarded as party politics but as defence of the Constitution and Fundamental Rights. Indira Gandhi accused them of receiving government funds and yet having the temerity to oppose government policies. This formulation was reduced to a written official note which she recorded as Prime Minister. She followed it up by ordering a roving enquiry into Gandhian organisations associated with JP. They had to be politically harassed. It led to a seven-year inquisition of over 1,000 voluntary organisations by the Kudal Commission set up for this purpose.

All these organisations got together and asked me to guide their defence against the Commission. Seven years of my life went into this Kudal Commission. I had to go through the Commission's notices to each of these 1,000 organisations and then the replies prepared by them. Then the defence lawyers called me for discussion in each case. All my other work came to a complete standstill. In the process, I developed some very vicious qualities. That is the only unfortunate perversion in my life. The working of my mind became very unpleasant. All my life I had done voluntary work and I found this was not a matter of voluntary choice. All the debates and arguments became combative. I was not very happy with this.

One of the fallouts of this was that I saw quite a bit of the government at all levels and although I had left politics, my political contacts got revived during the Emergency. Suddenly I found that I had become a Planning chap after the Emergency ended ! Uttar Pradesh was the first to make me a member of its Planning Commission. From there, Ramakrishna Hegde took me to Karnataka. Then Prafulla Mahanta made me a member of the Assam Planning Board. Later, I was made a member of the National Planning Commission.

Ques: Can you talk a bit about the Super Bazar experience ?

Ans: With the devaluation of the rupee came immense pressure from Indira Gandhi to do something soon to check the prices. Her close colleagues, Romesh Thapar and Inder Gujral, told her that I could do something about it. They came to see me but I was very reluctant and told them that I wanted nothing to do with the government after the Faridabad experience. But then Seshan, Private Secretary to the Prime Minister, called and said that it was a crisis situation and we must help out. So once again ICU plunged in.

Then Indira Gandhi sent a message that I should meet C. Subramaniam who was the Minister and was empowered by the

Cabinet to do whatever I wanted. I went to see him and his first question was how long my plan would take. I assured him that from the moment he gave me what I wanted, the store would open in 15 days. He said that it was impossible but I told him that it was my problem, not his. Then he asked me what we would need. I told him that we wanted a large space for the market—one lakh square feet. I suggested to him that next to Shankar Market was a new building that had not been allotted to anyone and he should try to get that. He said "Done!" But having said that he then found that the NDMC (New Delhi Municipal Committee) would not give the building. So he threatened that he would issue an ordinance and take away the building. We got the building in 24 hours!

Then we needed a bank that would finance Super Bazar. No bank would give the money, so he flew in the Syndicate Bank chairman, T.A. Pai, who said that we could issue cheques up to Rs one crore without waiting for formalities!

The moment he gave this assurance, I asked for the third assurance: that the government would not interfere and that I would not be required to pace the corridors for every little decision. I reqested him to name one officer with whom we could interact. So S. Venkitramanan who was special assistant to the Minister was named. Both Subramaniam and Venkitramanan were true to their words. They did not interfere at all. Rather, they helped at every stage. We had to employ 1,500 people at short notice, buy supplies worth crores. MPs and various people tried to push in their people and get favours, but Subramaniam erected a steel door and said that he had given his word of honour. In those 15 days, everybody got charged and transformed.

The scheduled date of opening was July 15. When Venkitramanan came to see the store on July 13, he was aghast—there was nothing inside. But the entire ICU team stepped in and they performed miraculously, beyond even my imagination. Subramaniam did do one favour for me. Indira Gandhi was to open the Super Bazar. He had made this commitment to her but I urged him to break that commitment because we had decided that the store would be inaugurated by the first customer who entered it. He convinced her.

The store was to open at 5 p.m. It opened at 4 p.m. because the police came and said that they would have to resort to a lathi charge because there were huge crowds milling around. I said to them: "Have a heart. How can a store open with a lathi-charge ?" We came racing down from the 5th floor and saw the unbelievable crowds. So we said: " What is so sacrosanct about 5 p.m. , let's open now." While the crowds were jostling, to their utter delight, the doors were thrown open. They rushed in, broke the show-cases. Our architect C.H.S. Jhabvala stood there and cheered and said that it was like breaking a champagne bottle ! He set the tone for us by saying that he had never built anything that had been broken by the people's enthusiasm. So that was the story of Super Bazar.

Ques: Everybody who was associated with ICU during its early years talks about the special magic of the organisation. Can you elaborate on this ?

Ans: We were rebuilding India. One foot had already been in the freedom movement and we just stepped into this. The total excitement just cannot be recaptured. There was electricity in the air at that time. The reason that I and many others came around Kamaladevi was that we were all charged with that electricity; some to a lesser degree some to a greater degree, but we just had to do something. That is why that period was known as a period of volunteers. Nobody was looking at their careers. It was only later on in ICU that people began asking the question: "What are our future prospects?" And we used to be baffled by that question. We found it to be the most irksome question. We used to say: "India's poverty is your security. There's enough work to do." But that question never haunted us those days. Which is another way of saying that it was because of the electricity of the moment that we had the gumption to believe that we were building India.

The other thing that was different was that the way we were doing it made everybody feel welcome and feel that they had a contribution to make. ICU helped everybody to grow and become larger; to discover skills that they never thought they had. It did not limit anybody. We were not a hierarchy, we were not a bureaucracy. For the most part, the spirit remained one where you wanted everybody to be content and satisfied. This is what they used to call the "ICU spirit". It was like a family where people felt they could come and even share their personal problems and they would find support.

It was a wonderful experience. However, there was only one very cruel thing I did and I have never ever forgiven myself for this. I think I ruined the life of one of the colleagues in the Cottage Emporium. She was a divorcee and had remarried one of my classfellows from college. In the Emporium we used to have vigilance against shoplifters. This unfortunate woman was caught shoplifting. The Staff Committee recommended that her services must be terminated. She came to me and wept, and said that if this incident got known, it would ruin her life. I just couldn't figure out what to do. After she left my room the Committee members came and convinced me that we had to give deterrent punishment otherwise the integrity of this place would go. So in that dilemma, of the individual versus the institution, I had to let her go. I failed. I could not become large enough to save both the individual and the institution. Thereafter, she never came to see me but I have never, never recovered from that. I did not know what was the right thing to do, but I just know that what I did was the wrong thing to do. This is something that comes back to haunt me even now. That has been the most tragic decision which I took.

Ques: Why was it that ICU did not take root ?

Ans: It was never imagined by us that ICU should take root. We always saw it as a platform to be discarded when the necessity was over. That is why in the first 20 years when we had funds, the activities expanded—Faridabad, cooperative farms, Cottage Industries. ICU did not acquire any property. We had consciously decided that we were not permanent.

The most poetic warning to us came from one of the farmers, Bhagh Singh from Chhattarpur. It was winter and the floors used to get very cold in the Janpath barracks where our office was. We decided to buy some coir matting so that our feet would not freeze. The next morning some farmers came to discuss something. Suddenly Bhagh Singh, who was a big man, lifted me and said: "*Mubarak ho!*" (Congratulations!) When I asked him why the congratulations, he pointed to the coir matting and said that now the office had become permanent ! We laughed and laughed at that time, but in fact, that gave us a warning not to become permanent.

We saw ourselves as a child of that moment. Historically, we were coming from the freedom movement. We had a sense of obligation. For instance, the major impact in my life came from my parents and the number of years they had spent in jail. We knew that it was because of that generation, we were independent. For me, then, the private motivator was always my father's role. He never complained of the scratches of the struggle in his life and this remained a strong pivot in my life.

The prevailing spirit was very powerful. There were many others working with us—there was Narendra Datta, Som Benegal, Bharat Sahai, Sitaram Goel, Raj Krishna—they were all very, very strong characters who had their own views and personalities. Idiosynchratic, if you like. But that was our strength. We were not just factory-made products, all of equal size and weight. Ordinarily no one could believe that we could work together as a team. What bound us was intangible but it was a strong bond. Whenever we went as a group somewhere, there was a presence that ICU had arrived. It lasted for quite a while. We kept on being recharged.

Ques: Did you ever move away from ICU ?

Ans: There was only one moment when I left ICU, but that was for just a few hours. In 1954, I went to Bihar with JP to see the Bhoodaan movement which was at its peak. I stayed there for 3-4 weeks. I walked with JP through the villages and actually sat through one of the meetings where land was distributed to the landless. Vinoba's slogan that we used to shout when we went to the villages: *"Sabhi bhoomi Gopal ki"* (All land belongs to God so why not share it with all His children) was a very powerful slogan. It used to have a tremendous effect on the people. The voluntary response that it evoked, to give, to share, was amazing.

I will never forget that meeting when land was being distributed —an acre per family. At the end of that distribution process, it became clear that one family had to go without land. There was not enough to give to all the landless. This landless labour looked forlorn. JP apologised to him and told him that efforts would continue to get his one acre in the next round. At this stage, one of the landless labourers who had received land, got up and said: "Give me only half acre, and give the other half to him." Then another, and another got up and said the same thing. JP said one acre was already too little and tried to assure them that the man left out would definitely get one acre the next time. But they would not listen. They insisted that they would share what is available now, then and there. When I came back to Delhi, I gave a talk at the Delhi School of Economics organised by K.R. Narayanan and V.K.R.V. Rao. I said that while the "economies of scale" plagues the economists, we should also think about the ethical scale, which is evident when a man says that he cannot live with one acre if someone else is left without anything at all. In our notions of economies of scale, this dimension never enters. To me that whole experience was like an enlightenment. I was gripped.

JP asked me to join him because while thousands of acres were available, they needed people to organise the distribution more scientifically. I told him I had to go back and consult ICU but during the train journey from Patna to Delhi I had decided to join Bhoodaan. I talked to Kamaladevi. She kept quiet. Then I got a message from her to see her in the evening. She was there and so was ICU's Vice President Srinivas Malliah, my fondest mentor. Suddenly she said: "Here is the key. Since you are leaving ICU, why don't you lock it up and take the key?" That's all she said and then she walked out of the room. But that act of hers came as a shock. She forcibly brought out to me my responsibility towards ICU and I saw that I could not just abruptly go away. Moreover, by that time my association with Kamaladevi had turned into such a bond that I realised what she was also saying was that if I left, it would be like splitting her. So I stayed back.

Ques: If you had to set up ICU again, would you do it differently at all ?

Ans: You see, we never set up ICU. We registered a piece of paper. Then the activities just grew out of pressures from the agricultural workers, the refugees at Faridabad, the artisans, the craftsmen, the weavers the slum dwellers, the consumers. It went on and on. So this is not a story where things were planned. That is why it was not meant to be an organisation to take roots; it was not set up according to any blueprint, but with the idea that that moment in our history required everybody to pitch in. The only thing I would say I'd do again, is that if there was a moment like that, and the responsibility was put on my shoulders, I would do it, but exactly how, would depend on the circumstance and the community in question.

❐ ❐ ❐

Two

"Our connection with our society is very tenuous. We have a fine heart, we have a love for the people. But that alone doesn't work."

— *Dharampal*

Ques: Where did you spend your boyhood years ?

Ans: I was born in Uttar Pradesh in Muzaffarnagar district in a small town called Kandla. But I lived mostly in Lahore because my father worked in the Imperial Bank there — or what later became the Reserve Bank. My schooling, therefore, was mostly in Lahore in a DAV school. Then I went on to college there and studied till Intermediate. It was an ordinary childhood.

In those days, in UP where we came from, engineering was supposed to be very important and lots of people used to go in for that. Rourkee College was the main institute at that time with a good reputation. My father thought I should try for that and so from the age of 18, in around 1940, I moved on to Meerut and joined college for two years to get my B.Sc. degree. However, I didn't go to an engineering college, because it was around this time that I got more political.

Ques: Were there any family influences to set you on this path ?

Ans: Around 1920, my father was part of the non-cooperation movement. Perhaps this influenced me — I'm not sure. He was at Benaras Hindu University when Mahatma Gandhi asked a whole lot of students to leave their college and join in the movement. My father also left. Then, in 1930 the Lahore Congress Session was held and I remember my father taking me there. I was small and was just wandering around there where I must have seen and heard Mahatma Gandhi.

Then around 1930-31 there was the Bhagat Singh case and I remember many of us boys demonstrated and engaged in other such activities. So all these events were happening around us. From around the age of 16 or so onwards, I remember starting to read a lot of things very seriously — even Trotsky! Reading was a very old habit. We used to have this Punjab Public Library which was on the way to my school where I used to go regularly from the age of 12 or so. I must have read a lot, and read various kinds of books.

Around 1942, I left college and joined the Quit India Movement. Nothing very prominent. I got involved with what was known as the Centre of Underground Command of the All India Congress Committee. We operated from Bombay. I was a kind of messenger boy. There was this very important man called Swami Anand who looked after me in Bombay, arranged for my stay and other things.

Around this time I also got interested in cooperatives, not in the Indian Cooperative Union sense, but in the sense of community — in the community living of ordinary people, not special people, not refugees, not elite, not the kibbutzim of Israel. In 1943, I was arrested. After release I went and lived in a rural area of Gorakhpur district. A friend's father was a manager there, of an agricultural farm of around 1,000 acres or more. But it was not a community type of thing. It was a commercial farm. Still, I lived with them because they knew me and they wanted to keep me safe and away from trouble. I stayed there for about one year.

Then, around 1944, some friends of mine had met Meera Behn (Miss Slade) who was thinking of starting an *ashram* called Kisan Ashram in North India near Rourkee. These friends said I must go and help her. I was reluctant to got but they said that she wanted some intellectual activities started there for some kind of training in how people should use freedom, etc. So I went and then stayed on for 3-4 years. I worked alongside her and we were very close right up to the time she died in Vienna.

Ques: Can you elaborate on the work you did there ?

Ans: I helped in building the *ashram*. We had to construct mud houses with bamboo and wood. In the early stages, Meera Behn and I were alone in this and then later others joined in — not too many. Well, personally I don't think I did very much. She, on her own did a lot of things, she talked to a lot more people. She was a person of virtue; I was not — not at that age, anyway! When more people came in, some of them did some spinning work, some helped in medical care. But I really don't think I did much. Even in the intellectual sphere, maybe Meera Behn and I had some intellectual conversations, but otherwise I don't think I did much. Well, people came, we talked, etc. But that's it.

We did not actually start anything, in terms of training people or running a school or anything. Then she got more and more involved with the idea of cattle and the *ashram* at Rishikesh and the preservation of forests.

Ques: When was your first brush with socialism ?

Ans: Not really socialism as such. But I got to know the socialists from around 1946. I met Jayaprakashji first in Delhi. Meera Behn introduced me to him and we talked for an hour or two about cooperative farming — that time it was the Russian model of collective farming.

Then in 1947, I was introduced to Ram Manohar Lohia and later to Kamaladevi, because I was still interested in the community concept and cooperativeness as such. Their idea then was to have a cooperative type of rehabilitation of the refugees who had come. Now, in retrospect, I feel it was the wrong sort of approach. But I didn't realize it at that time; we were all very enthusiastic. It was felt that if these people who had been displaced, instead of becoming individual entrepreneurs, could be cooperatively rehabilitated, it would be great for the cause of cooperation!

For example, there was this group of 400 families from a place called Jhang in Punjab, and there was this young man called Mulk Raj Sethi who was their spokesman, who thought they should all settle together. That seemed to be a great opportunity of having a kind of rural cooperative. Kamaladevi was also taken up with this, and she went to Alwar, met its ruler, tried to get land, etc. There was land available somewhere near Alwar, but money was not available. These people had some money — about Rs. 4-5 lakhs among them — but in the several months of waiting for the land, this money got finished. So the idea of a rural cooperative didn't materialise at all but some smaller land cooperatives did come up.

Around this time, an armyman mentioned that there were these communes in Israel. He gave this great picture of Israel. But how to go to Israel in those days? There was only one way we knew — go to England and from there go to Israel. So I went to England and stayed there for one year during which time I did a variety of things. I joined the London School of Economics for some occasional lectures on diplomacy, etc. I went to agricultural labour camps. I also got married to an English girl who was in the army and who taught in the school.

Then while returning, both of us went to Europe and then to Israel. We had some invitations that had been arranged partly by Lohia, but I don't think that was very necessary — the Israelis were very keen on other people coming and seeing what they were doing; they were looking for world support. So we went and lived on their first kibbutz — established by the Russian Jews.

Ques: Were you impressed by this ? Did the kibbutz adhere to your concept of community living ?

Ans: I was impressed, but realised that this was not for us. You see this was something created for a very special reason. People of one State who were kept apart for ages and ages, had been brought together and this was a means of keeping them together. For instance, at this kibbutz what they did was that all children from the age of 6 weeks to 18 years were kept together away from their parents (who could meet them for about an hour or so a day). But the people who looked after these kids spoke only Hebrew. So even when the parents wanted to talk to their children, they were compelled to learn Hebrew which was a language that had gone out thousands of years ago.

Now this kind of a thing would not have worked here that was my feeling then and is even now. Maybe under some compelling reason, if we were under great stress or if we're surrounded by enemies and there was a grave need for survival, then it might work.

Anyway, from Israel we came back to India but the community idea had still not gone from my mind. By this time, Meera Behn had moved to Rishikesh and she had got some land from the government on a long-term lease and she gave a part of that for a kind of commune. It was here that we created a village of 60 families who came from the nearby area. These were very poor people. We had brought together people from the hills and people from the plains and *brahmins* and *chamhars*, and it was a mess. I mean, we didn't really think it through. I got them to build their own houses. We thought it would be very good but it just didn't click. It does not work this way. It takes ages to build a community, and you see we had no resources. The village is still there, called Bapugram, a few miles from Rishikesh towards Haridwar. Many of the original families moved away; some have stayed, but it has gone the way of other villages.

Ques: Why do you think this attempt failed ?

Ans: Well, one was the caste system—*brahmins* and *chamhars* living as neighbours—that was an error on my part; I forced them to do it. The other reason was that they had lived at such a low level that they were not keen on having big houses, a big plot of land, which they were compelled to do. We had some different, funny designs and it was just messed up.

Ques: When did you work with the Indian Cooperative Union ?

Ans: Before I went to England I worked with the ICU. Initially, they put me in charge of the set up. Lohia was also there in some way, helping, suggesting, etc. But then he cooled off. Kamaladeviji was there. I did the work for a while but after some time I told them I couldn't manage it, that I would look after the community part—the rural community—but not the rest. I just felt I did not have the ability or capacity to handle it. There were plenty of other youngsters who were very enthusiastic to look after that part. So I worked on the community part where Gopiji was the important person, really.

In 1954, I went to England again and came back in 1957. That's when I had a talk with Lakshmi Jain and he told me about the concept of the Association of Voluntary Agencies in Rural Development (AVARD) and asked me if I was interested. Something seemed to be interesting in it so I thought, let me see.

I joined and moved around the whole country for 2-3 months, meeting various people and it seemed to me that it would work out. We got the organisation registered at the end of 1958 and it started working with about two-and-a-half people in it! I was with AVARD till 1964 and through this work I saw a lot of the country. We did some good studies on panchayats, etc. I asked a lot of questions about communities, about cooperatives, about the initiatives or non-initiatives of the people.

Through all this I realised that we were all wrong—that the picture was quite different to what we had thought and that we knew nothing about our people at all. And this includes all our great leaders, like Jayaprakash Narayan, our Prime Ministers—they didn't know their people.

Now I'll tell you an interesting story that happened in Sawai Madhopur. We were there to do a study of the panchayati raj system in Rajasthan which was the first State to adopt it around 1958 or so under the Balwantrai Mehta scheme. R.K. Patil was the leader of this team of about 7-8 people. Someone told us that there were some irrigation tanks there. So I asked if anyone was doing anything about it. They said that they maintained them. I wanted to know who actually did—was it the panchayat? The people said no, they themselves maintained the tanks—the people to whose farms the water went. When I asked why the panchayat did not do this work, they said it was not the panchayat's work. When I asked what then was the panchayat's work, they told me the panchayat's work was "development", but this was their own work. And when I asked them what was this "development" they told me that "development" was something the government did for them! So in this manner, I asked a lot of very basic questions and came up with some startling replies because of which some of our officers got very distressed. It was the same throughout India.

Ques: When did your interest in community villages deepen ?

Ans: In 1962, when I went to Puri once where I met the chairman of the Zilla Parishad and we got talking. He told me some interesting facts about villages that were there some 50 years ago. I asked to see some of these villages so he called the Block Development Officer (BDO) and I was taken to a village called Veer Narsingpur—a very ancient village, a very beautiful village, no less beautiful than any European village, clean, with many facilities, etc. The community sense had decreased a bit over the years. New government laws that had been introduced brought in concepts of land to the individuals, to the cultivator, etc.

I learnt that this was a *brahmin* village and I thought may be this is why it was kept so well, but later I was told that this was not so; that there were also some fisherfolk villages which were as beautiful. After that I travelled widely in the country and what was established was that in 1805 in Tanjore, out of some 5,000 villages about 1,700 were community villages. I got interested in this idea and I went around and saw several villages. Of course, these villages had deteriorated a bit because time had taken its toll, but the fact remains that we used to have such villages earlier.

This was when I moved out of other interests like cooperatives, voluntary agencies and so on, and went into quite another age. Now my mind retains only all that; it doesn't retain anything else.

Ques: In retrospect, what do you feel were the strengths and weaknesses of ICU ?

Ans: I feel ICU could have built up its strengths. But the point was, what did it want to do? You see, basically, ICU was a spontaneous effort to solve some pressing problems. Which it did, within its capacity, its manpower, the intellectual talents available to it and so on.

Then, these people, who joined and had the technical and professional capacity as industrial, agricultural, trade experts, wanted to be established somehow—individually preferably, or if not, cooperatively.

But ICU didn't become a movement. We may have thought it would become a movement but maybe we didn't think enough of it. However, there were people in it with a great deal of experience which could at least give the Delhi area what it wanted. I think it became something which the middle class—or the elite group, or the ruling class—ran. We were not in the government, but we were still the middle class, part of the ruling class.

The other factor is that in India, somehow, things fritter away, they don't go too far. This is something unique to India of the 20th century (we were not like this earlier). The active period for any organisation is 5-10 years, but here, the quarrels start the very second day. This may be contested by our planners and sociologists, but this is my feeling.

The basic problem is that we were, and are, dealing with an alien area. These cooperatives, collectives, voluntary agencies, or now NGOs, these are all modern concepts from the West. We have become their offspring; we are not the offspring of the Indian craftspersons or the peasants, we have nothing to do with them; we don't know them. I don't think even Lakshmi knows them; I don't think P.M. Tripathi (of AVARD) knows them either; I don't know them. So our connection with our society is very tenuous. We have a fine heart, we have a love for the people, but that alone doesn't work; that will not deliver the functionality or the momentum. We may benefit some 1,000-10,000 people, but then we disappear. They may regret it for a few days and remember us for a while, but then it's over; it doesn't take root.

Ques: Does the problem lie in the fact that organisations like ICU do not, in the true sense, involve the people enough ?

Ans: No, if we are thinking in terms of the Super Bazar or the Handicrafts Emporium, then we do that job, because it is according to some other design, some other blueprint—but this is not the blueprint of the people of India—this is what I want to say.

Ques: Is this a fault of our education system ?

Ans: Yes, yes, we have become Anglicised. During the British, those Indians with some scholarship, wealth, etc., and who wanted some secure and safe life, went over to the British. The British, through design, made policies to see that literacy in the Indian languages should not go beyond a point. Their aim was to increase literacy in English. So they had a plan and in this plan they created a class which was nearer to them, so that when the time of handing over came, they could hand over to their disciples. And this is actually what happened. At least, this is how I see it.

So we have not become one society and I see no possibility of this happening in the near future. That is why the Cooperative Act, or the new Panchayat Act, or the 33 per cent reservation for women, etc., will not work.

Ques: What was the kind of research you did when you were with AVARD and then later on ?

Ans: During my work with the panchayat, I went around many villages, I saw that our picture of them as inactive, paralysed, etc., was completely erroneous. We didn't know. They did think for themselves, they did whatever was practicable within their situation. Now in retrospect, I can see that these people who were so poor, at least provided us with 95 per cent of our food—by their means, not ours (there was no Swaminathan then!). Yet we stamped them as ignorant, unthinking, etc. We should be whipped, all of us, including the first Prime Minister and the next Prime Minister, leaders of cooperative movements, leaders of AVARD, all of us.

Later, I came across certain facts. One was the discovery of the 1,700 community villages which had no individual holdings. Then, there was some startling data I came across regarding land tax during the British. All this led me to an investigation to find out what we were like around the year 1750. That was my quest and that has gone on. What I have found is that not only in terms of villages, but in practically every field, the picture was very different. Our villages were prosperous and very advanced. I have now written several books based on these findings.

But for the past 10 years or so I have not been very active in this research. I have been living in Sevagram. I have not been doing very much, just living comfortably! I can't go to archives and do all that any more. I can't cope with anything new now.

❐ ❐ ❐

THREE

"Even at this stage of liberalisation, India needs cooperatives."

— *Gopi Krishan*

Ques: How did you start working with ICU ?

Ans: I was brought by the Indian Army (as a refugee from Kashmir) from Srinagar to New Delhi, where along with my family I was asked to shift to the Old Fort Refugee Camp which housed at least 20,000 people.

When I was forced to leave Kashmir, I was doing my MBBS from a local medical college. In the camp itself, I started working as a social worker and, in a few years, became the senior assistant to the camp commander.

My experience with ICU has to be seen in a special light: from the day I landed in Delhi, I worked with commitment to tackle all the problems of the camp right from organising accommodation for several thousands of refugees, schools for the children, jobs for the people and guiding them to set up small businesses.

Perhaps I can attribute some of these qualities to my early education. At the Reverend Canon Tyndale Biscoe school where I studied, it was a regular practice to take the students out on camps to villages for two months. I was always a very enthusiastic participant of these camps. The teachers at the school were very committed to their profession and made sure that they inculcated the right values in us.

At these camps students were asked to help sick people, if necessary remove them to hospitals or generally help them. Students even helped the farmers in farming and building roads.

So these annual camps were the single most significant factor which helped me to develop organisational and leadership skills. Besides, the emphasis on the physical aspects of education like swimming, boating and cross-country runs was also important for cultivating a healthy outlook to life.

Ques: What did your work with ICU entail ?

Ans: The Rural Cooperatives that I worked with were essentially formed to rehabilitate refugees. The refugees belonged to all classes and professions. Some were skilled workers, others were artisans, mechanics, merchants, government servants and landless farmers.

Kamaladevi, a prominent national leader, who initiated the cooperative movement in the country, identified the landless farmers as the most vulnerable group among the refugees. During their journey to India after Partition most of these farmers had lost their cattle. The only wealth they had was seeds of the crops they used to cultivate.

Along with Kamaladevi, I was involved in searching for the land for the refugees. I was closely involved in the Committee for Land Allotment, headed by the Commissioner of Delhi.

In 1948, due to all our efforts, the development work for landless farmers started on a huge scale. None of us had any idea what a cooperative was. Under the leadership of Kamaladevi we shifted about 50 families to the Chhattarpur area and formed the Agricultural Cooperatives Multipurpose Society. Land was identified in and around Delhi and refugees were shifted to villages of Jaidhpur, Jhangola, Chandanhullah, Godaipur, Sultanpur, Tughlakabad, Tigri and Satvari. In these villages, ICU identified two types of land—the land owned by *patwaris* in and around the villages and forested land.

The way I went about it was to live closely with the people so as to understand the power equations within the community and the village set-up. Besides the *patwaris*, the local inspectors can also impact land transactions. It was my job to keep a watch over these communities and manipulate possessions in favour of the landless, and the Land Allotment Committee. It was a difficult task to make people understand the advantages of owning and cultivating land jointly. In each village we tried to allot the land to each multipurpose cooperative society and then arrange cultivation and agricultural equipment for the villagers. There was also the problem of soothing the animosity that inevitably built up among the local villagers and the new migrants.

ICU arranged seeds and agricultural equipment and also made special efforts to get tubewells and ordinary wells organised. Organising irrigation facilities was perhaps the most complex work of the agriculture cooperatives. It was difficult to organise groups, to search out suitable land for wells and then organise actual digging.

There was also the problem of registering the cooperatives. Before Independence, the British had established a network of cooperatives which was similar to the network of credit cooperatives in the UK. The registrars and other government officials of the villages were reluctant to register the new cooperatives. It was my job to persuade the local villagers and officials to register these cooperatives as legitimate organisations.

However, sustained effort by the multipurpose cooperatives brought about good results. The villagers first set about growing food crops and soon they started growing surplus and through cooperatives they began searching for new markets to sell them. As the surplus of the initial few villages like Jaidhpur and Chhattarpur started increasing, news travelled to other villages and more people started showing interest in becoming members of cooperatives. Soon the rural economy became buoyant and villagers even started thinking in terms of growing cash crops. Besides the refugees, even local villagers started taking interest in the cooperatives and felt that the work for setting up a network of irrigation facilities could be taken up on a much larger scale and at a faster pace.

It was in the mid-50s that I started the massive exercise of lobbying for funds and seeking permission for constructing an eight-mile canal from Okhla to Jaidhpur which would irrigate many villages on the way and enable the villagers to sustain their four-crops-a-year cycle. Despite the interest taken by Nehru, it took us a year to cut through the red tape and get the project off the ground. However, by then the villagers in the area were aware of the advantages of working together through the cooperative. Once ICU arranged cement, bricks and technical help, the canal was constructed by volunteers from various villages.

Once the canal was built the real estate prices in the area increased by almost 500 times. Production too increased and farmers started growing cash crops including rice, wheat, sugarcane and vegetables.

Ques: What was the other work done by the cooperatives ?

Ans: Besides developing irrigation facilities, the multipurpose societies in the villages were also developing housing in the area. With the help of volunteers and material provided by ICU, each village had between 60-150 new houses.

By the end of the 1960s the affluence was visible and people were beginning to notice the area. Soon, the local authorities deputed a team of 35 engineers who set up base in Chhattarpur village and directed the establishment of a network of tubewells for drinking water in 103 villages.

But the engineers discovered that the area was not suitable for deep drilling. The then Prime Minister, Lal Bahadur Shastri, sent an ICS officer from Bengal who specialised in constructing special conical wells. Again, ICU motivated the villagers to dig the wells and provided them with meters and technology to build channels so that water could reach various houses.

As the irrigation and water network in the area started growing, people also started becoming more affluent and ICU felt the need to start yet another cooperative, Lift Irrigation Cooperative Society. Membership of this was on a voluntary basis. The idea was to help the villagers make optimum use of the irrigation network.

I was also involved with setting up many other types of cooperatives which were becoming increasingly important for the burgeoning rural economy. There were transport cooperatives, brick cooperatives, cooperatives for making roads and mobile medical service cooperatives, etc. Between 1950-70 I made many trips abroad specially to countries like Israel, Holland, Denmark and Sweden, where agricultural cooperatives had reached innovative levels of specialisation and were able to provide farmers with help in various fields, right from providing better and improved variety of seeds to new technology in agricultural equipment and irrigation.

Ques: What were the kind of problems that ICU encountered ?

Ans: When we started the lift irrigation cooperatives the idea was to make cooperatives for special purposes so that farmers could get sustained help in that particular field. However, affluence and prosperity were also changing the temperament of society in the area and cooperatives were increasingly being marred by petty quarrels.

In today's scenario, I feel that even in this stage of liberalisation, India needs cooperatives. However, bureaucratic red tape and loopholes in the government laws make it very difficult for cooperatives to become a viable enterprise. A subsidy or a grant should not mean that the government should stand with a stick in its hand. People who want to organise cooperatives get embroiled in interpreting the complicated cooperative rules of various state governments. Usually people who are poor and unemployed want to set up cooperatives, and they cannot be asked first to understand the rules. There are no large armies of dedicated workers who can make these people understand the rules. Despite some successful examples, most have failed to take off because the cooperative rules of the state governments are very complicated. The movement as such cannot succeed unless the cooperatives are made totally public enterprises. However, I firmly believe that farmers and agricultural cooperatives will always have an integral place in the Indian economy.

Ques: How long did you carry on with ICU ?

Ans: Although the country was successfully moving towards profit-making enterprises, I continued to be involved in the cooperative movement. Although many of my colleagues set up their own enterprises, I never felt the need to do so. My perseverance was due to Kamaladevi Chattopadhyaya. I got offers from various international cooperative unions, but Kamaladevi's charisma and commitment always held me back. I had to vacate houses when I could not pay enough rent, nevertheless I continued! All my life I allotted land and houses, but I never made my own house! I feel a little sad that the movement to which I dedicated my life has not sustained.

But working with ICU was a fascinating achievement. I feel satisfied with my life although I do not have any fixed deposits, houses, jewellery. I consider the movement as a life-time training.

When his Holiness the Dalai Lama came to India with one lakh people, ICU was asked for assistance. I was asked to go to Moosamari camp in Assam and there, I helped erect a huge refugee camp. Along with government officials, I organised fodder for hundreds of cattle that the Tibetans had brought with them. I even had to battle with the adverse coverage that the foreign media used to give to India's efforts at managing Tibetans. Acharya Kripalani and I gave a comprehensive report on the state of Tibetan refugees to the Ministry of External Affairs and special efforts were made to shift them to cooler areas.

Prime Minister Nehru had to make statements about the state of Tibetan refugees in Parliament. And since Nehru had assured Parliament that Tibetans were even being provided with employment opportunities, I was asked to make arrangements to generate employment for Tibetans. So, along with ICU and Kripalani, I organised training and production camps for Tibetans. We encouraged them to develop their own crafts and soon helped them manufacture paper. All this was despite the fact that the Tibetans and Indians did not have any common language! I even helped set up a school for the 15,000-strong Tibetan camp and a special curriculum was designed where information was given in Tibetan, Hindi and English. Soon the Tibetans started making exquisite carpets and along with the Dalai Lama, we set up Tibet House which started collecting the dwindling and rare Tibetan crafts and artifacts.

I worked with the Tibetans for almost 15 years, and often had to stay away from my family for as long as six months in a year. So, all the credit for bringing up our children goes to my wife Kamala.

Ques: What are you involved with currently ?

Ans: I now run a school called Geeta Ashram Vidya Mandir in Delhi Cantonment. The school is part of the Geeta Ashram Trust. It has been recognised by the government and recently I was informed by the army authorities that 300 families of soldiers were being shifted from Jammu to New Delhi after having served at the border for over six years. I am making arrangements to accommodate their 600 children in the school.

❐ ❐ ❐

FOUR

"Those were the days of idealism when we thought the cooperative and trade union movements would provide the solution for the country's problems."

— *Narendra Nath Datta*

Ques: What or who were the influences in your life that made you turn towards the socialist party ?

Ans: I come from the North West Frontier Province of undivided India and it was there that I got very deeply involved in the trade union and the socialist movement very early in life. We had all heard about Jayaprakash Narayan (JP) and the work that he and Ram Manohar Lohia were doing and I got very interested. I had just finished my school at that time but the interest had actually started much before that.

During the Quit India movement, Khan Abdul Ghaffar Khan, who was the main leader of the movement in our region, influenced us greatly. At that time we were in school and we were convinced that the British must go. We did not think of any other implications. It was only later when we started thinking about what would happen to the country—about the social and economic issues—that we realised there were no answers to that.

It was at this point that the socialist party had some programmes to offer. Some manifestos were drafted; JP had drafted two or three letters to freedom fighters and he had hinted at the type of society that should evolve after Independence. Some of these letters I translated from English into Urdu and we published and distributed them to a number of people. It was during this period that my serious interest in the socialist movement began.

In 1942, when the Quit India movement started, I was still in school. Even then we took part in that struggle, organising strikes, etc., even in schools. Ours was a Muslim majority school (95 per cent were Muslims) and we did have a lot of opposition from many other students who were dead against the Congress. But some Muslims were with us and we started agitating, closing the school and even picketing. Consequently, three of us were expelled from school in the final stages.

During this time when we got interested in the socialist thinking through JP's and Lohia's writings, I came over from Peshawar to Rawalpindi where JP was to deliver a lecture. We attended his public meeting and I must say we were all very disappointed because the man spoke very slowly, very softly, although his words were very fiery. I still remember, he was talking about arresting the governors and he said it so mildly, we thought this man is not going to do anything, he is only talking! But yet he inspired all of us.

Ques: When did you move to Delhi ?

Ans: Immediately after the partition, I came over to Delhi and was involved with the trade union and the socialist party here. In the trade union I was mainly working in the All India Railwaymen's Federation. I was the secretary and had to attend all the meetings throughout the country wherever the railway people were meeting.

Eventually, my family also shifted from Peshawar and we were immediately faced with economic problems. I had no job, my father had no job, nobody had a job. Since I was the eldest child I thought I should take up some work. When you're looking for a job you have to ask the people you know. I used to know Peter Alvares who was the secretary of the Railwaymen's Federation and a very experienced member of the Socialist Party. He was a very clean person and I've seen very few people in political life like him. Unfortunately, he is no more now.

He recommended me to Kamaladevi Chattopadhyaya who was also a member of the Socialist Party at that time. She was a member of the Faridabad Development Board which Jawaharlal Nehru was specially interested in setting up for the rehabilitation of the people who had come from North West Frontier Province. This whole refugee camp was being managed by the army, and at one point we thought we'll bring in civilian officers and withdraw the army.

Ques: How did your involvement with the Indian Cooperative Union (ICU) begin ?

Ans: Kamaladevi recommended me to the Faridabad Development Board and I suppose since I came from the same province, spoke the same language, knew the same culture, I was given the job of Camp Commandant. I liked that job. It was like looking after your own people.

That was the time that ICU got involved in the Faridabad activities. They were entrusted by the government to set up a few industrial units, to set up brick kilns, set up cooperative societies for the construction of the houses, getting the materials, etc. When they decided to disband the Faridabad Development Board, L.C. Jain asked me if I could come over to ICU. So I resigned from the Faridabad Development Board and joined ICU. This was in 1952 and that was the beginning of my association with the organisation.

Ques: Can you recall some of your experiences in Faridabad ?

Ans: There was the time when we persuaded the people to literally build their own township. They had to make it themselves. But they did not like the idea—they did not want to become labourers. So a group of us had to convince them about the importance of building their own houses, of laying the roads, etc. They argued that they would need to earn enough to support their families but since they were not skilled workers, they would not be able to earn very much. This was something that struck us too, especially since the size of the families varied. So we told them that we would subsidize their earnings, from 25 per cent to 100 per cent, depending on the number of family members. We told them that they must display their own initiative and then the government would help, but they should not depend on the government completely, for all time to come. They were convinced, finally.

I have one outstanding memory of the love and affection earned from the people of this camp. As the Camp Commandant, I had to distribute cash dole once a month. Every disbursement was about Rs. 2.5 - 3 lakhs. There were no offices—we used to sit in the open with just a tent pitched in that sandy area full of of *mehndi* fields. The refugees would form a long queue, come one by one, present their cards which I would scrutinise. Then I would give a pay order and they would collect the money from the cashier sitting nearby. One day while the disbursement was going on a sudden and huge dust-storm started. Our tent was blown away. The storm was so intense, we could not see a thing, and the entire cash was blown away.

When the storm subsided, I was in a real quandary. How were we going to account for the money? Would anyone believe us? I had just one option. I called all the people and told them what had happened, and I appealed to them to please go around the camp and collect whatever money they could find.

It took them about an hour or more but at the end of it each and every note was collected and was brought back to my table. Not a single rupee was missing! I just started weeping at that time. These were poor people who were starving at that time, but with a simple appeal, see how they acted. Where will you find such people anywhere today? Whenever I repeat this story to anyone, nobody believes me. They say this can never happen. But I know it can; it happened to me at the Faridabad Camp.

Ques: Did things move smoothly for ICU at Faridabad ?

Ans: I became ICU's organising secretary for Faridabad. We had a lot of activities there. But around 1953 we came into conflict directly with the government. There was one Minister at the Centre —Ajit Prasad Jain—who was not very well-disposed towards ICU and he created all sorts of problems. ICU, especially people like Kamaladevi Chattopadhyaya, said that we were there to help the government, we were not running an industry or something. Around this time there was a showdown and ICU withdrew from Faridabad.

Ques: Where did you go from there ?

Ans: I was then transferred to Delhi where ICU had taken over the management of the Central Cottage Industries Emporium (CCIE). Initially, Cottage Industries was run as a department of the government. But then they got stuck and requested ICU to take over the complete management. It was then that this phenomenal growth of the Emporium took place. I was secretary of ICU, with the CCIE and one of the secretaries of the Cottage Industries. Then the handicraft development suggestion came up and a survey for All India Handicraft Development was done. All this was done by teams sponsored by ICU. As a result, the All India Handicraft Board was set up.

I was actively associated with the Cottage from 1953 to 1973. When ICU took over at Cottage, there was rapid development. From a sale of Rs. 2.5 lakhs a year, it jumped to about Rs.7-8 lakhs. ICU did extremely useful work for the craftspersons and a number of cooperative unions throughout the country. Special preference was given to buying from them and providing special marketing facilities for them. That was the time that we got more involved in that.

Ques. Why and when did you move from the Cottage Industries to the Super Bazar ?

Ans: Around 1966 when the first devaluation of the Indian rupee took place, Indira Gandhi initiated the idea of Super Bazar because everyone was very worried that prices would shoot up. So the idea emerged that consumers should have (access to) at least one big store where prices could be kept within reasonable levels through direct purchases from manufacturers, as far as possible.

L.C. Jain called me up in Jaipur where I was on holiday and when I came back he told me about the idea of this cooperative store. L.C. Jain was the president of this store and we suggested a Board of selected people—from Hindustan Lever, Tatas, etc.—people who were known in their field. They were taken on the Board. I was taken as the first General Manager. At that time I was still on the rolls of the Cottage, so I went on deputation to Super Bazar.

That was extremely useful work as a cooperative. It was a tremendous job—we employed over 1,000 people, we had to make contact with a number of suppliers, and retailing systems, accounting systems were to be introduced. It was a very, very tough job too with about 18-20 hours of work in a day. We had done 18 hours a day in Faridabad also, but this was a challenging scheme. You see, those were the days of idealism when we thought the cooperative movement and the trade union movement would provide the total solution for the country's problems. Unfortunately, nothing like that happened.

But the Super Bazar did a great job and there were other similar stores that sprung up elsewhere in the country too. When we started off there was one in Connaught Place. Then we had two main branches—one in Patel Nagar, one in INA. Now, in Delhi there are more than 100 branches. All State capitals came up with a branch but of course, these were independent, sponsored by the State governments. Wherever we could help them in training, etc., we provided those services.

Ques: How long did things remain ideal at the Super Bazar ?

Ans: Initially, the Super Bazar was a totally cooperative venture. But later on it got into the rut of a government department. Members were enrolled; no meetings were called; government began to nominate the board of management. And then came the tussle of the politicians—who should become the chairman, etc. All the local politicians one after another started making their own appointments. And it went on in that way.

It was quite a shock. I was with the Super Bazar till 1969. Then I went back to the Cottage and then on to Ganesh Flour Mill's —another cooperative that the government had taken over. I was there till 1976. But I saw the changes in the Super Bazar even while I was there. The politicians had taken over and made a complete mess of it. The objective with which it had been set up—that it should be a cooperative institution in which members will have a say in all that happens—nothing of that sort happened. The initial period was a promotional one and all those people on the Board at that time were not personally interested. They were people with a distinct professional calibre. But later on, the people, who were nominated on the Board, were interested commercially in all these activities.

Ques: Was governmental interference a major stumbling block ?

Ans: Well, I wouldn't say that. You see, it depended a lot on personalities. For instance, when Kamaladevi was presiding and people like L.C. Jain were there, they had powers of persuasion; by their reason, logic and arguments they could overpower the petty thinking of government officers. But once these people moved away, the persons placed here by the government became all in all. There was nobody to confront them.

The Cottage Industries also ultimately changed and it became a total government undertaking. No one from ICU was left there any more. The only fortunate part of the Cottage was that it developed so well and it started generating its own sales ... like the Super Bazar where their sales are now in crores and they too are making profits.

But now the politicians have taken over in the cooperatives. It is the big people who are raking in the benefits. The people who are actually involved at the grassroots are not getting any benefit out of it. The government nominates the Board in most of the cases. It is considered a source of political patronage—if you cannot accommodate this fellow as a Minister, you make him the president of one or the other cooperative federation. How can the cooperative movement function like this? I remember when Sanjay Gandhi was very prominent, he made a mechanic—one Arjun Das—the vice-president of the Super Bazar. Everyone started wondering. This was just political patronage.

Ques: What would you say had changed over the years, for such a situation to arise ?

Ans: You see, those were the times when people were wondering what would happen to the country after Independence. There was a certain amount of idealism, although we all knew the problems—the country is huge with a tremendous population, etc. But whether we were going in the direction that we should be going, that was the important issue.

We thought that at least drinking water should be available in all villages; that everyone should have some employment. But nothing happened. The whole thing got vitiated after Nehru's death, and when Indira Gandhi and others came, it became a struggle for power all the time. Although people like Indira Gandhi and Rajiv Gandhi had their own ideas—I'm not doubting their intentions—they couldn't do much. Perhaps they were not up to the mark, or the problems were too big for them, and then it all got mixed with the personal lust for power.

Nehru himself was such an idealist, he could inspire idealism in others. But then he too had too much on his hands. I remember once when we had a conflict with the government in ICU—during the Faridabad days—Kamaladevi arranged a meeting for a delegation from Faridabad (including myself) with Jawaharlal Nehru. We went to his house to see him and we told him exactly what had happened. He probably agreed with us and was probably unhappy, but he could not do too much about it. You see the Ministers then ran it like a government project and there was no particular idealism involved there. Whether a cooperative movement was being built at Faridabad or not hardly meant much to them. Ajit Prasad Jain, for instance, was the last person to understand the spirit behind the cooperative movement.

Ques: On hindsight then, would you say it was misplaced idealism ?

Ans: I would not say it was misplaced idealism. I would say the people at the helm, including ourselves, failed to inspire sufficient number of people to see our point of view and join in. At that time for the younger people coming out of college, the important things were jobs, competition, etc. You see, career and idealism were two completely different things. Unless a JP or a Gandhiji came and told people that commitment was more important to build the country, it was going to be very difficult. But after Gandhiji and JP, there was no one around to inspire. I would say there was not a big enough leadership. I think it was a failure of the leadership to inspire people to come forward.

If Gandhiji could not have inspired people, the whole freedom movement would not have been possible. Before the Partition, I remember, once Gandhiji gave a call that he wanted one lakh volunteers for seven lakh villages of India, so that at least one volunteer could look after seven villages. I wrote a letter to him in Urdu volunteering my help and I got a reply in Urdu with his signature, accepting my offer, and saying that they had made a note of my name, etc. You see, such was the inspiration that when he gave a call, he got immediate response. If you have such people, then the country can be built in the way it should. That state, unfortunately, is not there now. Today's atmosphere is such that somebody may come and be able to motivate the people, but not inspire them.

Ques: Do you feel that there is a need for an ICU in today's scheme of thing ?

Ans: Yes, the need is there. Under the guidance of some selfless people—whether in the cooperative or the trade union movement or any other socio-economic movement—the country can go forward. The need is very much there. At the present moment there is not much happening.

The new economic thinking is not very clear at the moment. If globalisation brings in foreign investment and by virtue of their speed and industrial growth, if employment is created and certain economic prosperity comes to the rural areas, then that may meet the objective of the people's upliftment.

But whether this will actually happen is very difficult to say. Because all foreign investments have their own primary motive—profit. They are not coming to serve us. The risk is, if we start to have less and less say in the running of the country. It will all depend on the calibre and intelligence of the people who are dealing with the foreign investors, that while balancing the future of the country they don't lose sight of the people's needs. If globalisation means that all these industrial giants have a say in our economic policies and our political affairs, then God help us. So in concept, a body like ICU is important today. I would say, if not one ICU but a number of ICUs in every part of the country spring up, then it might be possible. Then there will be some safeguard for the country. Otherwise it will remain an academic question and a mere historical document.

❑ ❑ ❑

FIVE

"The most important lesson is that cooperatives have to be independent. The first thing that needs to be done is to free cooperatives from the clutches of government."

— *B.L. Dhar*

Ques: Can you speak about your early life and your initiation into the cooperative movement ?

Ans: I was born in Srinagar in 1928. I was educated in a missionary school and studied there up to matriculation. I graduated from the local college the year that India was partitioned.

In October, 1947, Kashmir was attacked by Pakistan-supported tribals. They almost reached Srinagar before the Indian Army arrived, stopped them and threw them back. At that time efforts were made by the National Conference to organise some resistance to the invaders. There was great support for it. A highly organised militia was formed and a large number of young people, including college students, joined it. I was one of them. Since I had some training in the use of arms, which was rare in Kashmir at that time, I was nominated as the in-charge of about 100 young men. We were given preliminary training for a few days in the use of .303 rifles and were sent to various villages and towns in the valley to hold high the flag. This helped in restoring law and order and the morale of the people.

Very few militia members faced the armed raiders because by the time it got organised, the Indian Army had arrived and had very little use for the militia except for gathering information and providing some guidance to troops during reconaissance. The army helped in restoring law and order in areas vacated by the raiders, and assisted in recovering the looted properties of people who had left their homes during the raids. Meanwhile, a popular government of the National Conference was being set up. By the end of 1948 the militia was organised as a regular force and people who had joined it were offered regular jobs in the Para Military Force. I, however, opted out of it.

As a consequence of the tribal raids and the closure of the main road to the Kashmir Valley (Rawalpindi-Srinagar Road) trade between Kashmir Valley and the outside world came to a standstill. This continued through the winter months, after the raid of 1947, when the only other outlet (Banihal Road) was completely closed due to the annual snowfall. The problem was further compounded by the fact that trade was controlled by a handful of non-Kashmiri traders who had fled in the wake of the tribal raids. This was natural as some of them had been killed by the raiders in areas overrun by them. So, in the winter of 1947-48, no exports or imports took place. Even essential commodities including tea, salt, sugar, kerosene were not available. There was no electricity as the only power plant was damaged by the raiders. Some quantity of salt was air-dropped and extremely small quantities (a few grams per family) of salt were distributed among the people. Other commodities were just not available.

With the collapse of the distribution system, an alternative system had to be developed. On the advice of Aga Syed Ahmed, the government decided to re-organise the entire trade by setting up cooperative societies. A Cooperative Department already existed but it had no experience. Its only expertise was of running a few small credit cooperatives. It was, therefore, decided to recruit fresh staff to organise these Cooperative Societies. About 10 new persons were recruited to help the Department to set up the cooperatives. I was one of them. Till then, I had never heard of cooperatives as I had not studied economics either at school or at college. It was by chance that a friend of mine introduced me to the Registrar of Cooperative Societies who thought that I could help in spite of my ignorance. Thus, I became a junior officer in the Cooperative Department. In between, we were sent for a year's training to Pune to learn the tricks of the trade. But this was much later. Initially we had absolutely no training. I went straight from militia to the cooperatives!

Kashmir already had one fairly good distribution system for cereals, rice, maize, etc. This existed since World War I. So what we did on joining the Cooperative Department was to organise about 300 primary multipurpose cooperative societies in Kashmir over the next year. But they were initially meant for taking over this business of distribution of essential commodities. A Cooperative Society was organised in four to five villages. Few Cooperative Societies were also set up in Srinagar for each locality (*mohalla*). We set up a shop in each locality/village. We got the goods mainly from outside and set up a central organisation with a central warehouse (Kashmir People's Cooperative Service) where all these items were stored and then distributed to the regional centres and from there to the individual cooperatives. I was involved in this activity, along with others for about three years. We established most of the cooperatives in a record time of about six months to eight months, without any experience. But we could do it because of the enthusiastic support and cooperation from the local people. People collected small amounts and each society had about 400-500 members. The government also gave some money to run the stores. Initially they distributed only essential commodities, but later these societies also distributed more items, including agricultural inputs. Then they started distributing loans and also marketing agricultural and horticultural products, which is why we called them multipurpose cooperative societies.

These were the first multipurpose cooperatives in the country. As these cooperatives were very successful and popular, politicians started praising them as one of the important developments in Kashmir, which had a direct impact on the people's lives. So most politicians, particularly in the rural areas, got involved in these cooperatives. Most of them later became MLAs and Ministers, but initially most of them started as secretaries of these primary cooperatives.

We, from the government, organised these cooperatives and advised them, told them how to do things; how to keep accounts, how to handle business, and how to keep money and get money from the banks. But they were the people's representatives and they became Presidents and Secretaries. They were paid some nominal remuneration of about Rs. 200 a month. At that stage, practically everybody who was anybody in Kashmir was in the cooperative movement. However, this movement was mostly confined to the Kashmir Valley, the State of Jammu and Kashmir was much larger. I continued in Kashmir up to 1955.

Ques: So you actually got into the cooperative movement accidentally ?

Ans: As I have already told you, I had never heard of a cooperative before joining it. At that stage I was merely looking for a job. After joining it I realised that organising cooperatives to set up distribution systems was important for the morale of the people. It was only after working there for some time and seeing the public support and response that I got quite enthusiastic about it and really worked very hard.

Ques: What were the principles or guidelines on the basis of which the Jammu and Kashmir cooperatives were run ? Were they similar to ICU or other cooperatives in the country that existed then ?

Ans: At that time I had not heard about ICU. Basically, in a cooperative organisation everybody has a single vote regardless of his equity or investment. It is a democratic organisation. In cooperatives, you have one person and one vote. It does not matter whether you have 10 shares or one share. That is the main difference. You have equal votes. Suppose I have 1,000 shares and you have only one share, you still have the same rights as I have. The only thing is how much you deal with the cooperatives; suppose one's dealings, as a member, with the cooperatives are more, one buys more or sells more or borrows more from the cooperatives, then the profits are distributed in terms of how one patronises the cooperative, besides some nominal return. So, that is the basic organisational difference between a cooperative and a private company. Cooperatives are really based on people and not on capital.

As I was mainly involved in organising and running marketing and distribution of consumer and agricultural inputs, I had very little knowledge about ICU. Kashmir, as you know, is famous for its handicrafts and as part of supporting the growth of Kashmiri handicrafts, cooperatives of artisans were organised. They supplied goods to the Central Cottage Industries Emporium (which I later learnt was part of ICU).

In Kashmir, up to the early 1950s most government jobs were held by Kashmiri Pandits—a community to which I belonged.

Kashmiri Pandits mainly worked for the government and they were disproportionate to their actual numbers. With the changeover to a popular government more and more Muslims, even with lower qualifications than required, were recruited in the government services. They were also given accelerated promotions over the heads of their senior Kashmiri Pandit colleagues. So sometimes, people who once worked under you, were promoted over you. That was one of the reasons why one was not feeling very comfortable there. They did not say anything. There was no problem with the people. But this was natural. I think, it was going to happen naturally because they were in a majority and they had held very few jobs. Therefore, whenever new jobs were created, they got them. During this time, a lot of people from my community left Kashmir in search of better opportunities outside. I also had some personal reasons because my family was mostly in Delhi and they wanted me there.

In late 1955, I came to Delhi. Since I had previous experience of working in a cooperative, I looked for a job in cooperatives. I knew that there was a Cooperative Department in Delhi in the Ministry of Food and Agriculture. Somebody suggested that I should talk to them. I did and they offered me a job. I was interested but not eager. I felt that unlike my earlier job I would be a cog in a large organisation, with very little initiative to do anything.

At that time, I was staying with my brother who was teaching in the Delhi School of Economics. I met Prof. Raj Krishna, who was a friend and a colleague of his. I told him that I was looking for a job, and of my interest in cooperatives. He said he knew one person, Lakshmi Jain, whom I should meet. I agreed and went and saw Lakshmi. I thought that since most of the people in the Cottage Industries were women, Lakshmi Jain was also probably a woman! I went in and he was sitting there and I suddenly saw a man with large eyes. It was a bit of a shock to see him. He said that Raj Krishna had told him of my interest in cooperatives and that ICU had a programme of rural development and cooperatives which would experiment with new types of cooperatives. He explained the project at some length. He asked me if I would be interested. I said I would be. He was very enthusiastic about this project and asked me if I was too. I said I was not excited, but would do my best if he gave me the job. That is all I could promise. I don't normally get excited. I wanted to think about it because I did not know whether I should go back to Kashmir. In Kashmir, although the job was not very big, we were very important. But, this was not so here. So, it took me some time to think it over. There was some pressure from the family also because they were very eager that I should come to Delhi. Finally, I decided to join, and did so sometime at the end of March, 1956.

Ques: How involved was the American Cooperative League in ICU ?

Ans: The Cooperative League was only providing some technical and financial assistance for some ICU projects. ICU comprised many things. At that time, it ran an Emporium, some collective farm cooperatives, handloom societies, and a medical programme in rural areas. Besides the showpiece Central Cottage Industries Emporium, ICU had also carried out a very large rehabilitation programme of refugees in Faridabad, about which I learnt later.

Ques: What were the tasks you were involved in at ICU ?

Ans: On joining ICU, I was told that I might examine the possibility of organising a federal union of existing cooperative societies in Faridabad. So, I went and saw the cooperatives and met some of their members. It did not look feasible because these people had already settled down. When they were under stress the cooperatives were very cohesive; once they got rehabilitated they had lost interest in cooperatives.

As a part of its rehabilitation programme, ICU had also set up a number of joint farming cooperatives. They were provided land, farm equipment, finances, etc. Initially they were supposed to have worked as collective farms but once the members, who were mostly refugees from Pakistan settled down, differences cropped up and these societies disintegrated. Later a detailed study was carried out by Raj Krishna for ICU which came to the conclusion that this type of organisation was not practical. At that time (1958) it created a big controversy as there were a number of important government officials who, after a visit to China, had stated that cooperative farming societies were the answer to the problems of India's rural population.

As the cooperative farming societies failed to deliver satisfactory results several alternative options were being considered.

One of the main problems facing the rural development programme was non-availability of credit to the farmers. If a farmer wanted a loan, he was asked to provide collateral or security. Where was the security? Now, the security can be offered only by a few big farmers and not by most of the farmers who have nothing to offer. So it was getting very restricted and whatever money was coming in was going only to the big farmers. That was the system. Based on our experience it was felt that the cooperative and other organisations were not able to provide any meaningful help to small and marginal farmers.

We talked amongst ourselves for nearly 6-8 months about what to do. We studied various projects in foreign countries and some of us also visited a few credit projects abroad. We came to the conclusion that a system be developed where credit could be dovetailed with improvement in the productivity of the farmer regardless of the size of his land holding or wealth.

It was, therefore, decided that we should set up a small community development project specifically meant for small and marginal farmers which would provide technical and financial assistance on the basis of need rather than the ability of the farmer to provide security for loans, etc. The emphasis of assistance should be to help the farmers in both technical and financial areas. The main features of this demonstration project, which was started in October, 1956 were:

1. It was restricted to farmers owning 15 acres or equivalent of dry land.
2. The assistance was to be based on the need of the farmer to improve his productivity, diversify cropping pattern, take up allied activities like dairying, poultry, etc.
3. The assistance would be based on a detailed farm plan prepared by the farmer himself with the assistance of the technical personnel of the project. These farm plans were also vetted by experts in different fields from various research institutes in and around Delhi.
4. No security was required for any loans.

5. The material assistance, to the extent possible, was provided not in cash but in kind, in the form of better seeds, fertilisers, draught bullock, cement, etc., for the construction of wells, field channels, etc.
6. This assistance was divided into short- and medium-term depending on the period over which such benefits were likely to result in an additional income/savings to the farmer.
7. The project staff provided assistance/guidance to the farmers for purchasing the necessary inputs with the financial assistance.

The first step was taken in 1956 when about 15 villages were selected in the Mehrauli area near Delhi. One of the reasons for selecting the Mehrauli was ICU's familiarity with it due to its other activities like joint farming society at Chhattarpur and the Rural Health Programme.

In the first year, only five villages were selected. In order to get to know these villages, community programmes were organised to eradicate rodents, some demonstration farms were laid out to demonstrate improved farming techniques to the farmers, besides the scientific use of limited water resources, effectiveness of use of better seeds, fertilisers, pesticides and other improved farming techniques. In fact in the first crop season (Rabi) only about 30 farming families were assisted. The project was expanded later to 15 villages. With the progress of the project, over the next 5-6 years a large number of activities, besides improving agricultural production and diversification of crops, were introduced including the development of new types of large diameter wells; *pucca* field channels; joint purchase of agricultural inputs; collective marketing of agricultural surplus; setting up of individual bio-gas plants; introduction of dairying; poultry farming; introduction and development of village industries, etc.

Although the project was quite small, it nevertheless, because of the new ideas being tested, received a lot of attention from government agencies, agricultural research institutes, foreign aid agencies, etc. In proof thereof, there were visitors at the project almost every other day.

Ques: How long were you associated with this project ? And what were some of these "new ideas" tested ?

Ans: I was associated with it up to about 1962. Some totally new ideas were tested and demonstrated. One of the things that we introduced, which received considerable attention, was a different type of well for irrigation. In Bengal, there used to be very broad and open type of community wells, with a circumference of about 100 meters. There were also tanks and ground and rainwater was also used.

We also introduced new concepts like cowdung gas plants, during the 1950s, organised some cooperatives and had a medical service which was started with some Canadian assistance. We had a medical van; there was a full-fledged doctor at Chhattarpur, where there is a big temple now. From Chhattarpur, the medical team used to go by rotation each week to all the 15 villages covered under the project. If we had serious cases, we would take them to Safdarjung Hospital which was the nearest hospital. We felt that these people needed medical care.

There was no work for some people, and so we gave them work on this new project like large diameter wells, introduction of poultry, multiple cropping, etc. We wanted them to be familiar with these new things. In this, we got a lot of support from others, for instance, people in the Agricultural Research Institute (Pusa Institute), New Delhi, who were interested enough to come and help. They helped in introducing new techniques, new technology and new crops.

Then, we developed and introduced poultry. Initially, the villagers did not agree to keep poultry, saying that they were vegetarians. However, there was a scientific and technical break-through in poultry development and raising poultry became popular once the farmers realised it was a profitable venture. They overcame some of the psychological barriers. We came to the conclusion that when you physically demonstrate something which is successful, farmers are clever and wise enough to accept it. Some of them may be illiterate, but they are very wise people because all the time they are taking more crucial decisions than us. They know that if they make a wrong choice, they may starve for the next three months, which is not true in our case; we would somehow survive. So, this is how new innovations were created there.

It was during this period that a Ford Foundation team was set up to advise the Government of India on increasing food production in the country. The team visited this project a number of times and was impressed with its performance. Some of the lessons of this projects were used in setting up Intensive Agricultural Development Programme (IADP) in specific districts in various States in the country. In fact, the ICU project personnel were used in training the first batch of officers, both administrative and technical, who were to man the IADP later.

Ques: What did you do after 1962 ?

Ans: By about 1964-65 the project had fulfilled its purpose by demonstrating the effectiveness of a new form of agricultural assistance based on individual farm plans. Some of the activities were handed over to the local community and others were taken up by cooperative societies organised by some of the beneficiaries of the project.

That was till late 1962. Then I went abroad because I was offered a fellowship in Sweden by the Swedish Cooperatives. Sweden is well known for consumer cooperatives. For the first time Swedish Cooperatives had invited an international group of about 30-35 young persons from all over the world to study Swedish Cooperatives and learn from their experience. We stayed there for about a year and a half. As a part of the training, I worked in some of their cooperatives for a few months. It was a part of the practical training; agricultural, consumer and agro markets, which was very interesting and rewarding. In theory, we were far ahead of the rest of the group. Then I came back to ICU but by that time, ICU had more or less concluded the rural development project in Mehrauli.

On my return from Sweden, L.C. Jain asked me to assist him in reorganising New Delhi Cooperative Store of which he had been appointed Chairman. It was headed by a Civil Servant and was run as all consumer cooperative stores were run. I had no executive powers but was to advise the Chief Executive Officer. He would listen to me but would always go by what the Registrar of Cooperatives and Delhi Administration told him and would take their permission before agreeing to anything new. Although we did make some progress, it was very slow. We helped in setting up a central store at Moti Nagar and started a large store in old barracks at Connaught Place where Palika Bazar is now. But the progress was very slow and there were considerable difficulties.

Ques: Was this the first time consumer cooperatives were being tried out here ?

Ans: India started consumer cooperatives almost at the same time that they were set up in Great Britain. These were, in fact, the first cooperatives set up in India; the first was set up sometime in 1904 in Madras, called Triplicane Cooperative Society. These consumer stores, by and large, were mostly small shops without any real impact on the market. Their number increased considerably during World War I and II, when there was shortage of consumer goods. These stores were mostly controlled by government agencies and confined themselves to selling only rationed items. Once the rationing closed they would close down.

Sometime in 1963, ICU had prepared a scheme for consumer cooperatives which would have some impact on the marketing of consumer items in terms of price and quality and would not be totally dependent for its existence on selling controlled commodities which you could not get anywhere else. This created a lot of other evils like black-marketing. In the cooperatives also, they would sell things as there was no real participation in these cooperatives. Some bogus cooperatives would be set up to get these rationed commodities from the government and sell them in the black market. These cooperatives really had no impact on the market, on prices, on anything.

ICU's proposal for setting up consumer cooperatives was lying with the government without any response. In June, 1966 the rupee was devalued and there was considerable resentment against it. It was feared then that, among other things, this would lead to inflation. At this time the ICU proposal on consumer cooperatives was taken up and the government showed interest in it. L.C. Jain was contacted by the government (C. Subramaniam was the Minister in charge of the Cooperatives), and they asked ICU to implement this scheme as it looked very promising. L. C. Jain agreed to this. But it had to be done very quickly and on a scale which would have an impact on the market.

So he called together a group of people, most of them from the various departments of ICU. I was one of these, as I had some experience in consumer cooperatives earlier in Kashmir and Sweden. Actually, I was on leave at that time in Kashmir. Suddenly there was a call from L.C. Jain asking me to return immediately to Delhi. I came back and he told me that we had to set up this store, that the government had accepted this scheme and we must go ahead with it and set it up in 15 days' time. It looked impossible. First, we had to organise a cooperative society. We prepared the by-laws, etc., and got it registered as a cooperative society in the last week of June, 1966, called Delhi Consumers Cooperative Society.

Then, we started looking for a place to set it up. We found a newly constructed building in Connaught Place belonging to the NDMC which now houses the Super Bazar. It was actually like the Mohan Singh Place, all small, small shops. So, we said, you give it to us and we would set up the store (which was called the Cooperative Store Ltd., better known as Super Bazar). Subramaniam promised all help and asked us what we needed. He had a Private Secretary, S. Venkitramanan, who later became the Governor of the Reserve Bank of India. He was asked to help us in getting various approvals, permissions, etc. If we had any problem, he would help. With the help of the Minister, we were able to get this building from the NDMC. Initially, the NDMC refused to give us this building. We finally agreed to pay them a rent of Rs. 5 lakhs plus one per cent of the profit. This was a lot of money at that time. Also, considerable expenses had to be incurred initially to remove a number of partitions to create space for setting up a department store. The only advantage which it had was its location, which was in the centre of the city. It had a large area—about 100,000 sq. ft. of selling space, six floors, including the basement; and on each floor there were four wings, each wing of about 16,000 sq. ft.

L.C. Jain had promised to set up this store in 15 days. It had seemed to be an impossible task but it was achieved within thc stipulated time! The group really worked round the clock to set it up. The people were mostly from ICU's various departments. We opened in two floors and the basement was used for stores, etc. It was opened on 15th July, 1966, on time—by a consumer and not by any VIP as was the normal practice. Consumers came in large numbers and we were very happy. It was a fantastic thing; houseful with a bit of confusion and a number of broken glass panes! They came to patronise the store and this continues even today.

One of the things we needed besides the building was money. We had no time to get money from the people because that would have taken time to mobilise. So the government decided that it would contribute Rs. 16 lakhs as share capital, but that was not enough to run the Super Bazar. We wanted loans for working capital. We approached the State Bank of India. Bank representatives came and gave us a number of forms to fill and arrange for security. We had nothing to show. So the State Bank of India was not interested. We again sought the help of C. Subramaniam. He asked T.A. Pai who was, at that time, the Chairman and Managing Director of the Syndicate Bank to give us a loan. He just asked how much money we needed. We said Rs. 80 lakhs. He said : "Done, but on one condition." And that condition was that he would open an office in the Super Bazar itself and the sale proceeds collected during the day would be deposited in the evening. He said he would keep the bank open in the evening up to 8.00 p.m. although normally banks closed at 2.00 p.m. He was prepared to open the bank even on Sundays as in the initial days the Super Bazar was open on Sundays also. And they really kept it open. They had to close at 7.00 p.m. and we used to deposit the sale proceeds from each department directly and they used to go on counting. That was the only guarantee they asked for. They were collecting every penny we collected every day.

Later, the Syndicate Bank provided loans to parties supplying goods to the Super Bazar against Super Bazar orders. Whenever we issued a fresh order for anybody they would give money to him in advance. So, they were also helped by Pai. He was actually one of the great supporters of the Super Bazar and the consumer cooperatives. Later the Syndicate Bank opened branches in all the main branches of the Super Bazar for the same purpose.

We had also set up a cell to help small-scale industries. Small entrepreneurs were provided information specifically about the goods.

The Super Bazar also gave them price preferences. A cell was set up which would inform all the people in the small-scale industry about the type of products the Super Bazar was interested in, the specifications and the prices offered. It helped a number of small-scale entrepreneurs.

Initially, we also had a large handloom department in which we sold cotton sarees below Rs. 15 per saree. We bought thousands and thousands of them, mostly from Andhra Pradesh and Tamil Nadu. They were sold in thousands. Rs. 15 was a very attractive price even in 1966. We would not sell any saree which was above Rs. 15.

Then, we also decided to fix our own prices. We would not go by the retail prices fixed by the big companies who insisted that their products be sold at this price or that price. Like Hindustan Lever saying that you sell Dalda at this price, etc. We bought at wholesale prices and we would fix our own retail price, which was usually below the market price. For this we set up a monitoring cell to get daily retail price from some important Delhi markets, like Khari Baoli, Karol Bagh, etc. The Super Bazar prices became standard prices so that they started being broadcast from All India Radio, just before the news in the morning. This was the benchmark against which consumers paid prices to private traders in Delhi and neighbouring areas. Even now, if you see the newspapers, they publish the Super Bazar prices every week.

At that time as part of our assistance to small entrepreneurs we developed and introduced a one-band radio. No large company was prepared to make and sell it. They thought it was not viable. We had found that most people generally listened to a local radio station. They basically needed a single-band radio only. So, we asked some small-scale manufacturers to do it. We found an entrepreneur in Bombay who agreed to produce a one-band radio which could be sold for Rs. 75 in retail price. It became popular and succeeded beyond anybody's expectation. It was sold in lakhs. It was unbelievable because we had put up its sales counter on the fourth floor in the household department. We were frightened that the building might collapse because there was such a crowd waiting for these radios! We had to move it down to the basement. We also persuaded the government that we should be charged only half the rate for radio licence as we were selling these radios at less than Rs. 100 per piece. The government agreed to this and charged only half the licence fee. In those days, there was a licence fee of Rs. 15 on a radio. So, they charged Rs. 7.50 only. And they also set up a post office counter at the Super Bazar to issue licences on the spot.

The other innovative measure we took was to open a drug store which would remain open 24 hours, seven days a week. This was the first time anybody had done it. We also took care tc guarantee the quality of medicines here.

We also were the first to sell pulses, etc., in pre-packed polyethylene bags on a large scale (which is now common practice everywhere). Moreover, all edible articles were pre-tested before packing. We had an arrangement with Lady Irwin College for this purpose. They would test each and every item at their laboratory. The Director of Lady Irwin College, Durga Deolkar, was a member of the board of the Super Bazar. She set up a laboratory where we sent all our pulses and other food items which were bought in the open market, and they would test it. Once they approved, we packed them in polyethylene bags for sale. It was done on this big scale for the first time.

Ques: In what manner did the Super Bazar expand ?

Ans: We had a sale of over Rs. 4 crores in the first year from our two outlets. That was a lot of money at that time in 1966. Then, we immediately opened one more store at INA Market. There was a building there which, again, had shops which were demolished to build a store. By the end of the first year, the Super Bazar was known for its price and quality.

Then we went to Rajendra Place. That was the first place where a department store was really built according to our specifications with a space of 20,000 sq. ft. on the DDA's land on short lease.. Jhabvala was the architect and he had earlier helped to re-design the Super Bazars at Connaught Place and INA, where he converted a large number of shops into a large selling area. He designed the store at Rajendra Place and since then a number of other cooperatives, even private parties have copied us. Both private entrepreneurs and cooperatives sought our advice on setting up and operating department stores. One of them was Century Bazar in Bombay.

At that time, every colony in and around Delhi wanted to have a Super Bazar. So, when a colony was built they would provide a branch of Super Bazar. Now there are about 150 of them. I was still at the Super Bazar when we set up a round-the-clock medical store in Irwin Hospital at the request of the hospital authorities. Then, similar stores at Safdarjung and AIIMS were opened.

To the extent possible we would get all our cereals, pluses, etc., from agricultural marketing cooperatives. We preferred the cooperatives because we did not have to bargain with them and there was no possibility of having made a deal with them. But it was not that we would buy only from cooperatives. We were also buying Rath, Dalda from DCM and Hindustan Lever, etc. We had both handloom and regular textiles. So, it was not set up mainly for the purpose of helping small-scale sectors or cooperatives, although it did help them. We gave them preference. But on the other side, we wanted quality and we wanted a price. That was important for us. It was set up mainly to help consumers.

The other advantage of the Super Bazar, as I stated earlier, was that it checked the price rise without government intervention. It was, as I told you, broadcast on the radio, every day. So whoever heard the radio from Punjab to Delhi would know that sugar was selling in the Super Bazar at this price and they had to sell it at that price because otherwise people would go to the Super Bazar. All of them may not have come but they could at least threaten the shop-keeper as it gave them some bargaining power. So, the Super Bazar became known for its standard prices for a number of products and saved a lot of money to the consumer directly or indirectly.

When the Super Bazar was set up, it received considerable publicity. Soon, attempts were made to set up similar cooperative organisations in other parts of the country including Bombay, Bangalore, etc. We had a stream of visitors from other States, from various walks of life, including universities, to see the Super Bazar and to discuss how they might set up one in their areas. One day even the President of India, S. Radhakrishnan, walked in, without any prior notice, to see it.

The Super Bazar now has an annual turnover of about Rs. 150 crores and it has been making profit right through, except for the first one or two years, and is still doing so. This is one of the few cooperative organisations which is running successfully.

Ques: How long did you remain with ICU ?

Ans: About 14 years. In 1969 I left the Super Bazar and started working with the Industrial Development Services (IDS), New Delhi. This was the formal end of my direct involvement with the cooperative movement. However, IDS has been helping cooperatives with ideas, as we have been consultants to some of them. For instance, we have provided assistance to NABARD and several other organisations in drawing up district plans to help in rural development and cooperatives. Personally, I have no direct involvement in the running of any cooperative but I keep in touch with various cooperatives through friends who still work there.

Ques: What would you say was the impact of your association with ICU, with cooperatives abroad, with your Super Bazar experience ?

Ans: As I told you, I spent the first 5-7 years with the government department of cooperatives in Jammu & Kashmir. The impact of working with ICU/Super Bazar, etc., was that it caused considerable change in my attitude towards the cooperative movement. Earlier, I was trained to think that without active government assistance and supervision there could be no cooperative movement. In Kashmir, a number of active politicians were working in cooperatives organised by us as a prelude to going into State Assembly and becoming Ministers. After joining ICU and working there for some time I realised that if people organise themselves voluntarily, they can do things better without much government help and supervision (which is not all that necessary). In India, there has always been a feeling that we should go to the government, that it is *maibaap* for whatever one wants. ICU demonstrated that people could stand on their own and succeed in achieving their goals.

We also demonstrated that new technologies could be introduced in rural areas by the farmers, etc. on their own without any government help. With the Super Bazar it was established that consumer cooperatives could be commercially successful—something very few government-run cooperatives had achieved. The Super Bazar also demonstrated that it could really make an impact, help not only members but the general public too, and its sizeable operation could influence the price of common commodities, improve quality of products in the markets, and no trader/businessman could ignore this.

In other areas like handlooms and handicrafts, ICU had again proved that voluntary cooperative efforts in production and marketing could significantly improve the quality of life of the producers, their products and create significant, large markets not only within the country but outside as well.

Ques: Do you think that cooperatives are doing enough work ?

Ans: I think cooperatives have done a lot of work and have succeeded in many areas. The cooperative movement has made a significant contribution to the development of the dairy industry (AMUL) and the sugar industry, urban credit societies, handlooms, handicrafts, fertiliser production, etc. Even the introduction of modern techniques in agriculture would not have been successful in raising agricultural production without cooperatives which provided credit, agricultural inputs like seeds, fertilisers, pesticides and marketing facilities. These are not well known because the media has paid very little attention to these achievements—media concentrates mainly on happenings in the urban areas, on large industries and mostly on politics.

The best and well-known example of a cooperative is AMUL. It was a pioneer in modern dairy development in India. It made a tremendous impact on the lives of its members and also helped India become one of the top milk-producing countries in the world next to the USA. There was nothing like this in the private sector at that time, when AMUL came up. Now it has spread all over the country. India is now emerging as one of the largest producers of milk. It is strong enough to take on international competition.

Ques: What about the controversy surrounding the milk cooperatives ?

Ans: That will always happen. Its success has created animosity amongst the private sector and international players who do not like to see it emerging as a very important player in this industry. But you have to see what type of impact it has. From what I have heard and read, it has created a lot of additional jobs; in fact, millions of jobs have been created all over the country. Women were empowered by giving them buffaloes—their own independent source of income. It has generated considerable additional income in villages. One can see that anywhere. I once went to a place called Bidar in Karnataka, as a part of my study for UNICEF and I found that in remote villages women were raising buffaloes and cows, collecting milk, selling it to cooperatives, generating their own income and running cooperatives. It was very exciting to see the modern dairy's milk collection centre in remote areas using the most modern technologies. Of course, Gujarat is far ahead in this. But do you know that these cooperatives have spread even to a State like Bihar which is quite backward in other fields? Maybe, in some villages, it has not been properly done. There may have been some mistakes. But these are possible in such a large movement. And mistakes happen not only in cooperatives; they can happen in any organisation. We should not forget that jobs were created, production was increased and we are producing something like 60 or 70 million tonnes of milk today because of the cooperatives.

Ques: Would you say that government assistance to cooperatives is imperative and only those cooperatives aided by government will flourish ?

Ans: No. Without the active participation of the people as producers and consumers, cooperatives cannot succeed only with government help.

You see, in the initial stages, the people who organise cooperatives have limited or no resources. Somebody has to provide funds, not necessarily as charity or subsidy but as loans, as are provided to the public sector, private sector, industries, trading companies, etc. These were provided by the government as commercial banks, etc., would not grant loans to cooperatives, since they generally do not have assets at the beginning to provide security for loans. But in the long run, cooperatives do survive if managed properly. They are democratic organisations and must manage their own affairs. The government-run cooperatives do not generally survive once the concessions and assistance are withdrawn.

Cooperatives, which are totally dependent on the government, do not survive; because they are constantly on "life support system". Once it is turned off or slowed down, the cooperative is finished. There were millions of cooperatives during World War II which were selling controlled commodities. Once there was decontrol of these commodities, they all disappeared. The Super Bazar was not like that. It was not dependent on the sale of controlled commodities and government patronage. It had its ups and downs, but it survived because it was totally independent and consumers had developed a loyalty to it..

Ques: What are the lessons learnt from ICU ?

Ans: The most important lesson is that cooperatives have to be independent. The only cooperative which will succeed in my opinion is the one that has full support and patronage of its members, and will help its members in achieving something tangible. Whether it is a consumer cooperative, or a rural, or marketing cooperative, whether it provides fertilisers or technical help, it will succeed only when it has the loyalty of its members. Anything which is totally controlled by the government will not succeed. One of the biggest problems in India is that cooperatives are totally controlled by the government and very few decisions can be made by the cooperatives themselves. The first thing that needs to be done is to free the cooperatives from the clutches of the government. The law must change and cooperatives should have independence.

Today, cooperatives often have their own resources. There are a number of cooperative banks, particularly in urban areas, that have collected large amounts of money which have been deposited in commercial banks which, in turn, do not advance loans to cooperatives. So, some sort of an organisational change is also needed by cooperatives to help each other, like we helped consumer cooperatives or marketing cooperatives, which eliminates a lot of middlemen. That would help both consumers and producers. So, what is needed is that cooperatives must have an all-India bank of their own to pool their resources for the benefit of cooperatives.

You see, agriculture and marketing cooperatives are doing very well. Sugar cooperatives, of course, are there. But the problem with these sugar cooperatives is that they are highly politicised, because once the cooperative is formed and if it is independent of the government, they are taken over by politicians, particularly if the cooperatives have sizable operations. Then, they become more of a political entity than a real cooperative. Then, as has happened sometimes, there may be changes in the government and the entire Board of Directors may be removed and new one appointed. This is because they think that it is part of their privilege to control cooperatives also. This is the problem.

There have to be fresh laws; and government interference should be minimal. Its motive should be to promote the cooperatives, helping them a bit initially. I think some help is needed in educating the members about the cooperatives and in terms of financial support which they cannot get from normal financial institutions. At the first stage, a little help is needed. But once you are out of this first phase, then the government should back out. A cooperative does not necessarily have to be government backed. NABARD is now helping cooperatives; all commercial banks are supporting the successful cooperatives in the agricultural sector. It is government assistance which results in interference that needs to be eliminated.

❒ ❒ ❒

SIX

"There was a difference between ICU managers and ICS officers. ICU thought in a humane way."

— *Gurbachan Singh*

Ques: Where were you born and what are some of your early recollections ?

Ans: I was born in 1928 in the North Western Frontier Province (NWFP). My father was a shopkeeper. I was born and brought up in my maternal village so the influences in my life were from my mother's side of my family. My maternal grandfather (who was not a Sikh) had an uncanny physical resemblance to Mahatma Gandhi and his beliefs too were very similar to Gandhiji's. In our village, he was the only one who got a newspaper and everyone would gather around his shop to hear the news. If there was any news about problems affecting the people of India, he would literally cry. I spent most of my time in his company and naturally, my interest in politics began at that early age.

In our village the school was only up to the primary level, so I was destined to have only that much formal education. After that I too got into the family business. But my interest in politics continued and grew. Although the NWFP was 90 per cent Muslim, because of Khan Abdul Gaffar Khan's influence, the Muslim League did not have much of a base there and there was a great deal of communal harmony.

Ques: How were things after the partition ?

Ans: My mother had passed away. When the trouble started after the partition, my father took me and my three sisters and stayed in a camp at a place called Kamelpur, from where we hoped to cross over to India. I remember, once my father booked seats for us on a bus that was to go to India. Some 17 buses were going that day. Unfortunately, someone else paid more money and took away our seats. But we later learnt that out of those 17 buses, only three had managed to go across the border. Ten of the buses came back and the rest were stopped and the passengers massacred.

Some days after this, we got information that another train was going to India, so we took only those belongings that we could carry ourselves and we left on that train and came to India.

Ques: Once in India, what did you do ?

Ans: Well, we were first taken to the Central Refugee Camp at Kurukshetra. Here, the Ramakrishna Mission was actively involved in helping out. I too volunteered to help in their work. Later, we were moved to a Delhi camp. But we had a lot of demands. Life was not easy for any of us and we were very restless. A group of us would go and shout slogans outside Nehru's house all night long. This was the only way we could make ourselves heard. We would sleep in the day and camp outside Nehru's house at night. Finally, many of us — Punjabi refugees from the NWFP—were arrested and taken to the Central Jail. In this jail, I met Narendra Nath Datta for the first time. He had been arrested in some other connection in Delhi and was also lodged here.

Once we got out of jail, we began discussing what was to become of us, and where we would go. At this point the government told us that there were two industrial townships coming up—one in Faridabad and the other in Rajpura—and we were asked to decide where we wanted to go. Some of us went to see Faridabad—it was a complete jungle there. But still we liked it and more so because it was close to Delhi. And that is how we—the refugees from the NWFP—moved into Faridabad.

Ques: Were things much smoother after this ?

Ans: No. There were a host of problems here too. We had won Independence but there was still a lot of conflict in the attitudes of our people, in their way of thinking. The ICS officers used to think in their own way, the Congress workers used to think in a different manner. So there was no convergence of thought on most issues. It was just that Nehru would dominate everyone's thinking and take the final decision and no one could contradict him.

Our camp was an army-run camp. But soon the government came up with the issue of how long it could supply the refugees with free rations. Not forever. So the Ministry of Rehabilitation decided that in Faridabad, whichever family was allotted a tent would be given Rs. 500 out of which it would itself build a *kucha* house. Not just this, but all the roadwork and everything else too would be done by us. None of us had ever done this kind of work before in our lives! The arrangement was that every person who worked would get Rs. 1.50 per day as daily wages and the Rehabilitation Ministry would give Re. 1 as bonus. So each person who worked would get Rs. 2.50 a day. And we all did this work quite happily. It had also been decided that every registered refugee would get a plot, regardless of whether he or she had a house back in Pakistan or not.

Mr. M.J. Bhatt was brought in from Delhi as the Chief Engineer and with the help of other people, a design was prepared and okayed for the houses, whereby a good two-room house could be built for Rs. 1,800. Narendra Nath Datta was our camp commandant. By the way, this house that I and my family live in now, the basic structure for this too was made by all of us from NWFP when the work here started! Of course, as the family grew, we added a few more rooms, but the basic rooms were made then, 48 years ago.

Ques: Is this where you first came in contact with ICU ?

Ans: Yes. The main intention of ICU, which was very active in Faridabad, was that all work should be done on a cooperative basis. I still recall my first meeting with L.C. Jain. Till then we had only heard about him and that he was a very important man in ICU. I was expecting a large and impressive man. Some of us went to the ICU tent which served as their office and asked a slim looking young lad there where we could meet L.C. Jain as we had something to discuss with him. When this young man said that he was L.C. Jain, we were really surprised! We sat with him and discussed various things and he talked to us about the idea of cooperatives. After hearing him out, I remember making one comment. I said : "So the government wants to lay the foundation of a socialist India over here." He was very pleased to hear that and said that I had understood things very clearly and that this was exactly what ICU wanted too.

ICU decided that when the township of Faridabad was built, it would be done cooperatively. In October, 1949 with the help of ICU, the work of Faridabad's construction began. In the cooperative scheme, naturally, there was no space for any contractors. We made groups of 10-12 persons each. An advisory committee of 11 was elected through votes (I was one of the five unelected members) and this committee then allotted tasks to all the groups. I found myself in the group that was assigned to work in the quarry. And then ICU appointed me as its labour cooperative organiser.

Ques: How did things progress here ?

Ans: The group system did not quite work out as was expected because some irregularities crept into the bonus payments that were being given. The chief accountant of Punjab came to look into the matter and it got into the press as well through stories in the *Blitz*. But this was the difference between the way ICU managers handled things and the way ICS officers would have handled them. Where ICS officers would probably have filed a case against those workers who had started taking extra bonus payments, ICU thought in more humane terms. The officers said that if we filed a case against these people, they will be stuck in courts and in lock-ups, and then who will look after their families ? They preferred to forget and forgive and instead try to find a payment system without loopholes that would work better. For some time the bonus was stopped, but many of the workers resented this, so then it was reintroduced in a more systematic manner. At this stage, N.N. Datta was made the bonus officer.

Ques: Do you have any specific memories of the work there ?

Ans: I specially remember one incident. Work in the township was gradually drying up. There was, perhaps, just enough work for 1,200 people in the industrial area. And the available manpower was about 4,500. A new chief administrative officer had come to Faridabad. One evening as I came back from my work tired and dirty, I found his peon waiting outside my door. He told me that the officer wanted to see me immediately. So I went to his office. There were some others there as well—O.P. Datta, the labour officer, C.P. Gupta, etc. The officer asked me to explain to him the system I used in assigning work to the people. I had worked out my own unique method which needed no roster but which I used to carry with me on a piece of paper in my pocket. I showed this to him and explained it. He was quite impressed and said that he found nothing wrong with it at all.

However, he did ask me if I could tell all the workers that from then on only one member per family could register to work in the groups. He said that these were the orders from the Minister because there was not enough work for everyone. I refused to do this because I was certain that this would create a lot of anger and resentment among the workers. So he requested me to try and convince the workers, but I said I would not do so because it was not a fair decision, and that instead, he should try and convince the Ministry.

One of the other men sitting in his room remarked that in Delhi labour worked for six annas a day and why should these people work for so much more. I turned to him and explained that these people were used to having a six anna cup of tea every morning before they began work. I told him that these people were not ordinary labourers and that they all had been used to a certain standard of living; that these people were refugees and, therefore, guests of the Ministry of Rehabilitation. After listening to all this the administrative officer told me that I should carry on my work as always and that he would try and talk to the Minister about it and get back to me in two days. From his office, I went straight to L.C. Jain's house and told him what I had said. I will never forget how happy he was that I had spoken out fearlessly, putting forth ICU's point of view on this issue.

Two days later the peon came to get me again. I went and the chief administrative officer received me with great respect and said that the Minister had agreed to what I had said but on one condition. There would now be some alteration in the doling out of free rations per family. I knew this was a minor adjustment for the sake of appearances, so it was quite acceptable.

Then after some days, the permanent chief administrative officer was appointed—one S. Barve, ICS. Now, as I said earlier, the perceptions and the point of view of ICS officers were quite different. After some meetings with all of us, he said that our work groups which comprised 10 persons each should be expanded to have 25 persons per group.

By now, I had enough experience trying to make cooperative ventures work and I knew that these groups could never work with so many people. I tried to convince him that this should not be looked upon as merely a bureaucratic or administrative matter but it should be looked at in the context of how people can best work cooperatively with each other. And keeping this in mind a group of more than 12 persons would be very difficult to handle. However, the bureaucrats did not agree. So, because of this (and some other problems that had been cropping up) I resigned and gave such a letter to Barve.

Then once again I went to L.C. Jain and told him that I had resigned. He asked me what I planned to do but I had nothing in mind—I had just handed in my letter without having thought of the future! So they absorbed me into ICU, this time to help in its agricultural cooperative. This was in 1952.

Ques: Why do you think things did not work out the way they were expected to ?

Ans: The one thing that went wrong, I would say, was the difference in the way of thinking and the beliefs of ICU and the refugees. The idea that was predominant in the minds of the refugees was that of trying to reach that same standard of living which they had left behind in Pakistan as soon as they possibly could. And to achieve this, they were prepared to do whatever it took—even if it meant going against the cooperative concepts. This, I feel, is one sentiment that ICU did not take into consideration.

I stayed with ICU till 1969. When I first came into ICU, I thought I would use my contacts with all the groups that I had worked with in Faridabad and work further with the cooperatives here. However, when ICU itself withdrew from Faridabad, that chapter came to an end. I then got involved with ICU's agricultural cooperatives—its cooperative farming programme.

In the context of cooperation, one incident stays very clearly in my mind. ICU had organised a huge conference on cooperatives in Delhi, at which Gulzarilal Nanda was the chief guest. All of ICU's cooperatives were participating in that meeting. I noticed that whenever the various members of any one cooperative talked and discussed among themselves, they always felt that the other cooperative was far more cohesive, more united, more "cooperative". I found this quite amusing. But I realised that, in fact, each cooperative had similar problems, but each one saw only their own problems and not the other's.

And over time, the cooperative nature of these societies started deteriorating and they stayed cooperative in name only.

Ques: What did your work involve at this stage ?

Ans: Around this time, ICU made me a "contact" man for the research team. So I had to be in close touch with the *patwaris* and others in the villages. L.C. Jain told me that all these years I had been a searcher; now I should try to become a researcher!

In 1956, the supervised rural credit project began. This was a pilot project of ICU for the marginalised farmer. I was given the responsibility for three villages where I had to identify those villagers who were most deserving of loans. It was very interesting work for me and I learnt a lot in that time. Over the years, working in the villages and interacting closely with the farmers, the one thing I did realise was that there was a tremendous gap between what people in offices discussed as theory and what actually happened in the field. In my own way, when I made observations of the way things really worked in these villages, I always shared them with the people from ICU and other officers and I believe it helped them in their planning and thinking too.

In this manner, till the end, I carried on with ICU, and my contribution was the information that I collected on the ground for the organisation. Much of this Raj Krishna used in his research too and I felt honoured to have been of help there.

After leaving ICU I went through very bad days financially. But somehow, we pulled through. Then for a while I worked with Lok Kalyan Samiti. Now I'm a retired man. And I do whatever little I can to help with my son's business.

❑ ❑ ❑

SEVEN

"Inspiration came from the need of the time — the need to do something for our country."

— *Swaran Datta*

Ques: Can you recall the days of your childhood and the influences that impacted you then ?

Ans: My family was originally from Multan. I came to Delhi with my brother when I was only six years old. It was when I was about 15-16 years old that I and a group of friends got interested in what leaders like Jayaprakash Narayan and Ram Manohar Lohia were saying. We were not allowed to go out by our families, but we used to listen to the leaders regularly and then discuss the issues they talked about.

Inspiration came from such leaders and the need of the time; the need to do something for our country. It was not so much the family but the atmosphere of the times, I'd say, that pushed us into this work. In fact, we used to fight with our families to go out and work at that time.

For instance, when Mahatma Gandhi used to visit the *bhangi* colonies in Panchkuin Road and when he held the 4.30 a.m. prayers, we attended them. We used to go out for *prabhat pheris*. I remember my greatest wish as a small child was to go near Gandhiji and touch him.

Ques: Did your family object greatly to all this or were they encouraging ?

Ans: I had lost my parents quite early and my brother who brought me up was not keen that I should continue studies. But I was adamant and I told him not to worry. Soon, I started to do a bit of work at the radio station. Then gradually I started attending socialist party meetings without my family's knowledge. The present Janpath was known as Queensway. This was where all politicians, social workers would gather to discuss issues about freedom, about the country's future, etc. There used to be study circles, meetings, etc., and I would attend these.

It was here that I came to know L.C. Jain and others. I was doing private college because I wanted to be involved in this work as well. I got to know Kamaladevi Chattopadhyaya here. She really loved me like her own daughter. She inspired me; she was my guiding spirit.

Ques: When did your association with ICU start ?

Ans: I was there from the time ICU started. I remember we used to have just one room then and we would sit on benches and trunks. Then Kamaladevi started taking me to the refugee camps where the women were working, making pickles, stitching clothes, doing cane work, etc. Gradually, we organised things and set up different societies, so that we could sell their things in the market and provide these women some money.

Ques: How were things at the refugee camps and what was the kind of work you did there ?

Ans: It was a very sad experience. I am still moved when I remember those days. These women used to cook their food, feed their families, specially the children, and then often there was nothing left for them to eat. They had left behind a lot of property.

I was managing the women volunteers groups at Kingsway Camp, then a group at Tis Hazari and at Daryaganj. Gradually, the work expanded so much that one person was needed for every camp. The procedure was that orders would be given to these women in the camp, and when they were ready, the volunteer would inform us. We would collect the items and then market them — the marketing was done through the Cottage Industries at that time.

Teji Vir Singh was then looking after the Cottage. We would stay there the whole day, sell as much as was possible and then take away whatever was not sold because at that time the Cottage was such a small shop that there was not even enough place to store the items. There were other small shops also and we requested their owners to keep the items.

The women at the camps did not earn much from all this. It was more an occupation. Of course, some of these ladies later on made a name for themselves in business, but at that time, life was very tough for them although they were getting some money from the government by way of cash dole.

Ques: Can you talk a bit about the family planning work that you were closely involved with at these refugee camps ?

Ans: Yes. You see, since we worked closely with the women, we thought this would be a good opportunity to talk to them about family planning. It was very difficult to make them understand that children are not merely god's gift; that they too had a role to play. This work too was initiated by Kamaladevi and then in our own way we tried to make the women in the camps understand what the need of the times was. Although the women were helpless to a large extent, they did understand what we were trying to say and they saw the advantages in what we were trying to tell them. In terms of their own health and from the point of view of their children's health too they realised that they needed spacing, that they needed time.

Ques: How successful would you say this work was ?

Ans: I think we were quite successful in spreading the message and making the women at least understand the importance of family planning. After all, don't forget that it was a new concept not just for them but for us as well. I was not even married at that time, but we did understand that if instead of six children you had three children then you would be able to give them better education, better food and clothing. The knowledge of contraception was not very clear to us, so we had to read a lot of books. But I liked the work and had a very good person like to guide me — I'm very grateful to her. I worked at the camps and other areas for 10-12 years. For instance, they started a small centre at Nabi Karim Mohalla where they used to have a medical help centre, children's education, women's craft activities. I used to work at this place from morning to evening. Many young people put up various cultural programmes in these areas too, so it provided a change for the people too.

ICU also invited some experts on family planning. The Ford Foundation, for instance, sent us an American expert, who used to visit us and show us how various educational aids like plastic moulds would help us to explain things better to the women. Often the women of the camps were too shy to come when the American expert was there, so they would come to me later and make me explain to them how these things would help them and where they could get the contraceptives. At that time, we would give them the contraceptives because ICU was distributing them so that the idea of family planning could be spread.

Then there were other activities organised like health shows for babies which were also arranged by the experts like Dr Hooder. For instance, we began incentives like prizes to the healthiest babies, etc. ICU also sent us Indian women doctors to help us.

Ques: What other work were you involved with at ICU ?

Ans: After some time Kamaladevi sent me for a three-month crash programme in social work at Western Court in Delhi. This included all aspects of social work — adult education, child education, health, family planning, etc., and instruction in methods of communication with people.

After this course, I was sent to Faridabad, where Narendra Nath was my boss and we got to know each other here. We got married in 1951. I was the head of the social workers' group there. Ashadevi Aryanayakam was already working there with the people, so Kamaladevi asked her to guide and advise us. Unfortunately, however, she did not like the idea because we were a group of young men and women working together — we were five women and five men. They called me for a meeting with the local leaders and explained that they did not want us there. I said I would go if Jawaharlal Nehru told us not to work there. But finally they understood our point of view and we continued working, although separately from Ashadevi's group.

Ques: What aspects of working with ICU stay most in your mind ?

Ans: Well, the selflessness of that core group of people in ICU was something different, something exceptional. People like Kamaladevi, L.C. Jain, Som Benegal and my husband — they all worked in a committed manner as a team. That kind of dedication and commitment is difficult to find now. It stretched to even personal level. Kamaladevi was also concerned about the health of persons working with ICU. You see, this kind of attachment and consideration you don't find now and that is why we were all so motivated to work for them so hard.

Ques: Do you think that an organisation like ICU can work today ?

Ans: Well, it's difficult to say. Priorities of the younger generation have changed. They have to struggle so much to survive in this world now. But still, even now I sometimes feel that instead of living in the cities if we can go to the villages, to the people, things will be different.

Of course, we don't have the stamina now at this age, but even so, if somebody wants similar work to be done, I will be the first person to volunteer. If there are selfless, dedicated people who inspire you and can bring out your best abilities and there is proper guidance, even at my age — I'm 68 now — I would do it.

❏ ❏ ❏

EIGHT

"Instead of taking from the government, we were giving them institutional frameworks to work upon and sustain."

— Kamala Rana

Ques: How long were you associated with ICU ?

Ans: I am a lawyer by training and have a diploma from Bombay's Tata Institute of Social Sciences. I was associated with ICU for over a decade and was involved in working in a number of cooperatives in and around Delhi during that period.

For most of my career with ICU, I was involved in the social welfare and community development aspect of the communities with whom I worked. In 1953, for example, I was given the responsibility of organising the community welfare centre in Malka Ganj and Kadamsharif areas of the capital. The main emphasis was on creating a better atmosphere in these communities, so that people could live in a more hygienic and progressive environment. I was actively involved in organising many activities in this area including pre-school education for children, health clinics and adult literacy classes. I always started with trying to know the people first, rather than teach them. I tried never to compromise on this point and was always keen to have meetings, organise fairs, indoor game space, etc. Since people from the lower income groups are terribly busy, I did not shy away from sometimes having even midnight meetings to get to know their problems.

I think I was an avid fund collector and a good "networking" person. In Kadamsharif, Najafgarh and Malkaganj areas, I was the first one to introduce CARE's milk distribution scheme. After a few days, I discovered that women, specially housewives, were using the milk powder to make tea. So I organised a few buckets and clean water and insisted that women and children, specially lactating and pregnant women, should come to the camp to drink milk.

While organising activities for women I always made sure that men did not feel alienated. So indoor games and adult literacy classes were usually mixed affairs, and we all tried to introduce health and sanitation and nutritional aspects in these activities.

Over a few years, I was made secretary of the social welfare department of ICU. My activities increased and many of the projects overlapped. My experience of earlier work in the slum areas helped greatly in my subsequent involvement with the rural cooperatives in areas like Mehrauli, Alipur, Chhattarpur and Fatehpur.

Ques: What was the work that you specifically did with the women's cooperative ?

Ans: Around 1957, I was asked to revitalise the women's cooperative in these areas. There were around four cooperatives — almost all of them around a decade old. Ten years of economic and political changes in the country had taken their toll, and the leadership was wearing thin. When I inherited the cooperatives, each had around 80-100 members. The women were mainly involved in activities such as paper making, *dari* weaving, *maṣala* grinding, retailing fabric and handicrafts, making uniforms for schools and police.

Most of them were feeling discouraged. Although they knew and were aware of the process of buying the raw material and turning it into furnished goods, they had not been able to tap larger markets. Most of the women worked from home and saw each other at occasional meetings when raw material was being distributed. Usually in each cooperative, a couple of women were calling the shots and others were either fighting with each other or feeling alienated. Records were in a mess and cooperative by-laws demanded that more and more registers be maintained. My experience in the slums had taught me that lack of nutrition, overwork and the responsibility of running a family usually leaves women tired. Here too, women were working hard, but they had no time to plan. I introduced the concept of rotational responsibility. Usually, a pair of women would be given a particular responsibility for a few weeks. Some, for example, were responsible for buying raw materials, others for maintaining one of the 11 fat registers. A pair was responsible for running the cash ledger. Divided responsibility helped and to a certain extent women became more accountable. For example, if the signatures did not tally, they would take the trouble to correct the situation.

Once the record keeping system started working, the women felt more enthusiastic. We have to remember that most of the members had hardly studied till class VI. They had to really push themselves hard to concentrate on the technical aspects of the cooperative by-laws and lock horns with the government inspectors. Besides, bad health and lack of nutrition sapped their physical as also emotional energy, and we, a handful of social workers, had to constantly motivate them to stay together. The cooperative that was making uniforms for the police was almost collapsing. The women had to be persuaded to maintain quality and collectively bargain for a better price.

My whole effort was to understand women's perception of the cooperatives, only then could I hope to reach them and motivate them. Usually, some women with more space in their houses provided a place for storing raw materials and packaging goods. I tried to liven up these places by organising there weekly tea parties, where women could exchange experiences, brainstorm about new retailing outlets and markets and most of all, discuss their domestic and social problems. Once a month, or so, there were brainstorming exercises where men were also invited and we discussed various issues: How were profits from the cooperatives being utilised? Who was making the optimum use of profits? What were the other areas where cooperatives or collective groups could be organised? Usually, these meetings were exciting affairs for the members. In villages, specially, news of such gatherings travelled fast and people helped in even organising exhibitions of finished goods of the cooperatives. Usually, in urban slums, it is difficult to make people come to such activities since they are busy, travel to work and live more alienated lives. In fact, during one of the rural cooperative meetings, the members floated the idea of forming a health cooperative. And the Chhattarpur Health Cooperative — one of the first of its kind — came up.

Ques: What, in your experience, were some of the lessons learnt vis-a-vis cooperatives ?

Ans: Several years of working in these cooperatives has made me realise that usually the institutions need enthusiastic external leadership for a continuous period. Only sustained effort from outside can restore the self-esteem of the workers. Social functions, interaction and money (profits) go hand in hand in infusing life into cooperatives and communities. Moreover, as technology becomes significant, people skilled only in handicrafts start feeling more and more discouraged. To organisers too their work seems deglamourised, insignificant. It, therefore, becomes even more important for the external leadership to remain more vigilant and enthusiastic. ICU's policy was to revitalise some cooperatives and then to move on to others. So in a limited period that I stayed on with these cooperatives, my effort was to give them as hard a push as possible so that they could go on for a longer period after ICU withdrew leadership and organisational support.

During 1958-63, the uniform cooperative did well. We had revolving funds of over Rs. 40,000 and women had become adept at dealing with Ludhiana textile and wool merchants. But at this critical stage, we at ICU were very vigilant that leadership within and outside the cooperative did not get politicised. Each meeting, therefore, had a clearly chalked out social or economic agenda.

While I was revitalising the women's cooperatives, I was also looking after other community welfare activities in the villages of Chhattarpur, Fatehpur and Sultanpur. Besides running adult literacy classes, pre-schools and crafts workshops, I also introduced sport activities and distributed skipping ropes, rings, cricket equipment and indoor games for the community. Special efforts were made to revitalise the creches and *balwadis* in the region.

Ques: Which cooperative would you rate as the most successful ?

Ans: The Chhattarpur Health Cooperative. This was started in collaboration with a Canadian aid agency and was supposed to run till the municipal hospital in the region came up. Almost 4,000 members from 10-15 villages registered for the cooperative. Since people usually do not take free services seriously, we had decided to take a membership fee of Rs. 6 per year. An injection cost Re. 1 and we charged 50 paise for medicines. The doctor visited these villages regularly and a trained nurse helped train midwives in the villages. The cooperative even had a van which could help transfer patients. I must say here that the success of the project largely goes to the far-sighted leadership of L.C. Jain. He and others envisaged projects and cooperatives which could be nurtured to grow big and then they were handed over to the government. So instead of taking from the government we were giving them institutional frameworks to work upon, improve and sustain. That aspect of successful cooperatives has to be remembered.

Ques: What were some of the other activities you undertook at ICU ?

Ans: One of my concerns was also to impart organisational and motivational skills to as many people as possible. So I tried my best to train people in accounts, record keeping, marketing, healthcare, sales, teaching, etc. As a result, I myself, over the years, picked up skills as a trainer. At ICU, besides my other responsibilities, I became responsible for training administrators, sales assistants, supervisory staff, accounts personnel, social workers, etc. This, I feel, is imperative for leaders of cooperatives — they have to be all-rounders and cannot shy away from any kind of work.

I then joined ICU's Artisan Welfare Committee, where I had to travel to villages, map the needs of the people, suggest solutions, institutional alternatives and submit the report for ICU and government inspectors. While others were working at increasing marketing outlets, etc., my specific job was to integrate the needs of children and women artisans with the mainstream effort.

Then from 1967-68, I served ICU as the Assistant General Manager at the Super Bazar. Essentially, it was what is now described as Public Relations. My job here included interacting with consumers, organising forums where consumers could file complaints about the Super Bazar and seek redressal. Initially, I began handling the consumers alone, by organising meetings. But soon the goodwill generated by these meetings attracted more customers and I had to involve more colleagues in these meetings.

Ques: After ICU what did you do ?

Ans: Well, ICU certainly had a great impact on me. I was always a "people's" person. Even now, I run a Thrift and Credit Society at Sangam Vihar which, perhaps, has the largest slum in Delhi. I still believe that an organisation like ICU can be revived to serve people in our country today.

❒ ❒ ❒

Nine

"What a world it was ! Offering very little in material, personal compensation but rich in the wide avenues of service to the dispossessed of society . . . . "

— *Som Benegal*

Ques: Can we begin with memories of your childhood and some of the early influences in your life ?

Ans: I was born into a poor but not impoverished family. My father was a rather petty municipal corporation employee in the old Madras Presidency. But he was by no means a petty person. Rather, he carried an enormous dignity in demeanour and character. His work took him to the various ends of Madras Presidency; consequently he was well-versed in Tamil, Tulu, Kannada, Malayalam and Telugu. And, of course, English and his mother-tongue, Konkani.

He raised a large family of his own—ten children of whom I was the youngest. He also helped (how, in his poor station, I don't know) others in the larger family around; various strands outstretching in various directions but unfolding when their needs arose.

My mother stood by my father in all the travails and felicities of life. They were both stubborn and yet compassionate. I mention this because they passed these traits on to me. There were other qualities also, virtues in those days but, alas, eroded over time and almost extinct now.

My father was a man of extreme non-violence but what is interesting is that he disagreed with Gandhiji, an apostle of non-violence. He was convinced about the beneficial rule of the British in India. He could not countenance Gandhiji's defiance of the British and the turmoil that followed. At that point, in 1932, when I was 10 years old, my father and I were ideologically separated. Incredible as it may seem, at that young age, the ferment of the times had gripped me. I had succeeded in enlisting my small circle of young friends, who later were to become distinguished citizens of free India, to join me in our crusade to rid ourselves of the British.

We, of course, did not fully, if at all, comprehend the ideology and dimensions of Gandhiji's electrifying lead to the nation in those days, 65 years ago. But it speaks for the shock waves it radiated that even we (barely beyond babyhood) could feel its thrill.

My father saw this with some consternation but seemed to have decided to let me go my way. But his concern for me was deep and abiding. Perhaps, because he was conscious of the anguish and agony I was going through as a result of the elephantiasis which I had inexplicably acquired at the age of five.

In those days youngsters had to wear shorts and not trousers. Consequently, I was subjected to taunts and jeers all around about my leg. The torment was not just the taunts of schoolboys around me; far greater were the jeers of the grown-ups one met on the street. Cars and carriages were few in evidence. In any case only the wealthy could afford them. Buses were scarce so one walked most of the time.

Ques: How did you cope with all this ? Did it leave you embittered ?

Ans: When you are young you do not have the consolation of philosophy to fall back upon. You take it on the chin—hard. But the trauma can result in two responses in later life. Some let it sear them to swear a vengeance on society for the hurt caused; others are led to promise to themselves that they will never cause any hurt to others as they had suffered. This is the revelation of compassion—the most beautiful and exalting of sensibilities. I consider myself blessed that I was moved along that path.

An escape from torment came in a rather interesting way. My brother-in-law, a man of great vision, and his wife, my sister, who greatly loved me, was a research doctor in Kuala Lumpur in Malaya (now called Malaysia). He had defied tradition and the sage advice of elders and decided to go East. A wise decision because he rose to high medical and intellectual levels. Without hesitation he agreed to take me to Malaya where I swore I would never wear shorts again, come what may. My gamble paid off. In the four years I was there I finished school—the best school even to this day—which taught the great principles of right behaviour and action, the spirit of camaraderie, *esprit de corps*. Those boys of those days—Malays,

Chinese, Indians, Ceylonese—are my staunchest friends even today after 60 years.

But above all, my brother-in-law, recognising the various stages of my growth in the turbulent times from boyhood to pubescence and adolescence, took me along with unimaginable sympathy and understanding. But he did something else of everlasting impress.

The middle 1930s were tempestuous times when ideologies were in clash—imperialism, fascism, Nazism, socialism, Marxism. In the West, the Soviet Union was an outcast; Hitler was much admired. Appeasement was in the air. But the Spanish Civil War inspired the cream of the cream of Western intellectuals to greatest action and creativity, infecting the atmosphere and spreading, in this case, the wholesome virus of resistance toward a looming World War.

The East was no less in turmoil. The Japanese inroads into Korea, Manchuria and onward through coastal China and further West into Indo-china had been seen with alarm but with a certain self-confidence mixed with disdain that the Japanese could never be a true menace to the might of Western, especially British, imperialism. What a misjudgement of the nemesis to follow!

It was in these tumultuous times, that my brother-in-law gathered me into a perspective of life which has dominated me through all the pathways I have tròd in my 75 years in this world. With an infinite understanding of my development, he guided me into a social vision which must inform all human endeavour: the impoverished of society before oneself. In caring for the last man down the line, put yourself lower down. A very sweeping vista indeed. Without a social vision, he said, life is not worth living—alas, an "altruism" as it may be called today, that has been shattered and turned upside down. Behind all this was, of course, socialist thought. The Left movement, meaning largely socialist, in contradistinction to communism or Marxism which also was widely studied and appreciated. The Spanish Civil War led to a great positioning of Left and Right forces and many rallied to the anti-fascist side. All this could not but influence me.

Ques: When did you come back to India and how did it feel ?

Ans: Returning to India on the 7th of January, 1939 was a traumatic experience. The stark poverty at the point of the ship reaching

Madras was numbing after the comparative affluence of Malaya. One had seen pockets of poverty in Malaya, masked by the arrogance and overlordship of the third-rate British rulers there. But this was a new experience. Its saving grace was the fervour of our freedom struggle which would erase, if not eradicate this blot on our society.

How naive we were then! How naive we have persisted in being after all these years. Indeed, how we have transformed ourselves from being naive to being so polished and finessed to change from doves to vultures of society. And our new leaders, not ashamed, but proud of their contemporary role of fleecing the nation while bathed in hypocrisy!

Ques: Did you get involved in the freedom struggle ?

Ans: 1942—"Quit India"—a pathetic revolution, mixed with people who went to jail and earned kudos (especially the Important Ones) and those who kept out, working out a revolutionary role of underground resistance, using crude elements of explosion which often blew into their own faces. Pathetic in today's context of AK 47s and RDX. But impelled by Jayaprakash Narayan's stirring "Letters to Freedom Fighters" that were smuggled out of jail.

I was part of it. But as the link between the underground forces between Delhi and Bombay. Shuttling perhaps, without glamour, was hazardous but in that moment of exhilaration of being part of a revolution was enough to carry anyone to a high of ecstasy. I will not burden you with what we did or of the great leaders of the underground that we helped. To detail this would be to be insufferably boastful. As in those days when we worked silently in the background, so now silence is a stronger attribute.

Many of us, including myself, watched with dismay as the events unfolded, leading to the disenchantment of an unacceptable concept of Independence and its attendant horror of partition and the shattering of all our dreams and aspirations.

It is interesting to note that as "the transfer of power"—so rightly expressed in contradistinction to "freedom" or "independence" —was nearing, some of us gathered together to form a group daring to envision a new India. Of course, this group, mainly of college students most of whom later achieved highest distinction not in power but eminence of excellence in moral and intellectual standing, foresaw and espoused the ideals of socialism, secularism and its most acute form—its emphatic repudiation of any discrimination of class, caste, religion or social and political division and strangely, to quote from its credo, "women's liberation"—a phrase unheard of then, but later to sweep the world.

Such then was the further accentuation of my views on life and my living. But to achieve this was not easy. Pressing needs and no doubt some internal weakness led me to join the News Service Division of All India Radio (AIR) in the immediate days of Independence. But the incongruity of serving in an organisation wholly repudiating the concepts of free expression, wholly subserving the ruling class, and worse, the outmoded ideas of bureaucracy which could not come to terms with the post-colonial dynamism of a democratic people's era—this incongruity became painfully ridiculous in time. With no compunction and with nothing tangible to enter into, I left AIR to walk into a wilderness and despair to the taunts of friends that there was no place in the world for altruism and impractical ideals.

Ques: How and when did you join the Indian Cooperative Union ?

Ans: My entry into the Indian Cooperative Union—in other words, the field of development—could be considered either an accident, coincidence or ordained.

They say that in moments of despair a door always opens. And so it was that after months of wandering like a lost soul, a door opened. A door into ICU, led by what was seriously and humorously called "a dedicated band of workers", with Kamaladevi Chattopadhyaya firmly and passionately at its helm and L.C. Jain its sure-handed navigator.

Between 1953 and 1955 while still in AIR, I had informally helped the Handicrafts Board and ICU—one in publishing a "catalogue" of Indian Handicrafts, the other with the "Report on Marketing and Production of Handicrafts". This report led to the radical change in the whole approach to crafts promotion and later, ICU's entry into the Central Cottage Industries Emporium as a trail-blazer, showcasing Indian crafts.

When I walked into the wilderness in 1955 after resigning from AIR, Lakshmi asked me if I would join ICU to help in the promotional aspects of the Emporium—its advertising, publicity, publications and public relations. It seemed a good challenge and also an opportunity to realise at least one side of me—to work without too much regard for oneself. There was this whole world of rural development, urban small producers, slums, social welfare, refugee rehabilitation and, of course, crafts.

And what a world it was ! Offering very little in material, personal compensation but rich in the wide avenues of service to the dispossessed of society—in village and in town, in the slums and among refugees displaced by the partition. Among them were poor, exploited artisans and craftspersons—a whole gamut of people "who needed help to help themselves", as the cliche went.

There was tremendous self-satisfaction and self-realisation in those exciting 15 prime years of my life. Those were perhaps the most wonderful years of my life, given no thought of personal career or material advancement. No one believed it then and no one believes it today that one could be so thoughtless and so foolish as to sacrifice one's life to this self-denial.

Ques: What were your responsibilities at ICU ?

Ans: My entry into ICU was, at first, received with much scepticism, and even hostility, by the senior personages who felt that I had come in as a friend of the General Secretary (that is, Lakshmi). It is another matter that when I left after 15 years, there was some regret and quite some reluctance to let me go. The whole face of development had changed. "Market-driven forces" (to quote a buzz word) had taken over and I had become a "dinosaur" (to quote another jargonism) !

But the first thing I did when I entered ICU was to give the Emporium an identity. That identity was the Bankura horse adapted in two-dimension (or flat) as the aspiring and inspiring logo. A new typography was given to the name of the Emporium. Its advertisements were changed from staid announcements of weekly goods on sale to intriguing, exciting invitations to come to the Emporium.

Later, I was tempted and drawn into the Craft Design Department, Showroom Display, Exhibitions, and also the first Art Gallery which tried to get artists and craftspersons to interact. Now, that gallery—"Kunika"—is forgotten.

At one stage, I was also asked to handle the administrative "management" of the ICU family in all its widespread wings, during the absence of Narendra Datta who went for specialised training to the Administrative Academy in Hyderabad.

But in all this, is the enduring, even nostalgic, remembrance that we all worked cooperatively in a cooperative, full of dedication. We did what we did for a cause. We felt it was a cause worth sustaining.

ICU as a voluntary non-profit organisation made path-breaking and innovative forays into economic and social development—a paradigm for others to follow. But nothing fails like success in India (and perhaps elsewhere too). Venal, rapacious, self-seekers interested only in their narrow interests have wiped out all the sterling achievements of ICU and reduced not only the organisation but the whole cooperative movement to a shadow, a grotesque caricature of its one-time grandeur. But that is the irony and tragedy of change. And yet the spirit which ICU engendered lives on, at least among those who carried it to its peak.

❑ ❑ ❑

SECTION II

TEN

"I couldn't tear myself away from helping the craftspeople of our country."

— *Fori Nehru*

Ques: How far back does your involvement with crafts go ?

Ans: When I came to India in 1934, there was hardly anything made in India. Isn't it strange that at that time no Indian craft was considered beautiful — only things imported from England and Paris. Women of the upper classes were dressed in French chiffons! My father and mother-in-law took me to a shop managed by two Parsi nationalist ladies who carried only materials made in India. So the first sarees I purchased were Indian made. My mother-in-law never wore anything but *khadi* and from her extensive travels in the country she brought me handloom sarees, so I never wore anything but sarees produced in India. Slowly I discovered the beauty around me. I got married in 1935; Panditji was in Dehradun jail at that time. Kamladidi, his wife, sent me a beautiful carved Kashmiri silver box as a wedding present. But from the jail Panditji sent a fountain-pen — one of the first, or perhaps the very first fountain-pen made in India.

Ques: When and how did you get involved with the Refugee Handicrafts and then later the Cottage Industries Emporium ?

Ans: It was the summer of 1947. There was murder all over the country. In Delhi it started on the 7th of September, that day a great friend of ours, Currimbhoy, was butchered in a taxi en route to Safdarjung airport.

On the 11th September I joined in the Town Hall "Emergency Committee" set up by the Government of India to help with the chaos prevailing in Delhi. I was the only woman in that office. The Chairman was the Commerce Minister, Cooverji Bhabha; the working head was H.M. Patel. The other regular members were Randhawa, the Deputy Commissioner, and Sunil Roy, the Superintendent of Police, who was the liaison officer between the Army and us. The government drew many more high-ranking ICS officers from the Ministries to work in the Town Hall. Those were the days of curfew.

The Committee wound up by the middle of October. I spent many a sleepless night thinking of the poor women, men and children living in the refugee camps in Kingsway.

What could we do? Gradually while talking to friends the idea emerged that we should tap their inborn knowledge. The women in Punjab know how to stitch and embroider. Why not set up something? Through dinner parties, receptions, lunches, we kept discussing these possibilities.

My mother-in-law, also a refugee from Punjab, was in charge of the last Hindu refugee camp in Lahore till the 28th of October when she arrived in Delhi to stay with us. She was appointed Honorary Secretary in the Ministry of Rehabilitation. Meharchand Khanna was the Adviser. It was a political appointment.

Around this time, with the help of Raksha Saran who worked with a team of ladies in the refugee camp, I started the idea of the Refugee Handicrafts Shop — and in what a manner! We had no shop, no place, nothing. I went to see "Pandit Brothers" in Connaught Place. The owner was Pandit Inderbhai Haskar. I entreated him to help the refugees. I asked for one counter in his shop which he willingly gave. In the meantime, we started taking orders from our friends for sarees, blouses, linen, underwear, etc., to be embroidered. On the 1st of April, 1948, the "portals" of Refugee Handicrafts opened at one counter of "Pandit Brothers" and we were amazed. Having announced by word of mouth that we were opening a shop, on that very first morning, we were swamped — people brought all kinds of clothes to get embroidered.

We had our counterparts in the camps. Sheela Puri was one of the ladies who used to come to "Pandit Brothers". She took from us cloth, went back to the camp and, a week or so later, brought these things back ready and embroidered. The sensitive craftsmanship of these village women from Lahore or Sind or wherever, who took refuge in Delhi had to be seen to be believed. The skills were inborn, you didn't have to teach them anything. In Punjab, at the birth of a girl child the women of the family start embroidering *phulkaris*. The richer the girl, the more *phulkaris* she is given in marriage. These very *phulkari* stitches and designs the women in the camps transplanted on to sarees and table linen.

The customers kept on increasing. The idea occurred to us that we should also have some readymade pieces for sale. So we purchased readymade items from the refugee women—they all got sold.

In this manner, our work grew and the business grew so much so that by the month of July, Inderbhai Haskar said to me : "Look Fori, I have no place for my own things. You women are sitting from 10 in the morning on my carpets (which were for sale) and no one can see these carpets." I went to my mother-in-law in despair and told her that we were going to be thrown out and requested her to try to get us accommodation. We were assigned an evacuee shop in Barakhamba Road where we remained till 1952.

Ques: Who were the others working with you on this project ?

Ans: I could not have done all this work myself without the help of Kitty Shiva Rao and Prem Bery. At this new shop, I was completely tied down. I had to be there constantly — to open the shop in the morning, to close it at 1 p.m., to open again at 3 and work till 6 p.m. My husband started getting restive and annoyed! Fortunately, my mother and my mother-in-law who were staying with us looked after the household and the children.

More and more women joined to help in the shop. By the time we shifted to Barakhamba Road we worked out a roster system. I did not want to handle money nor did Prem Bery nor Kitty Shiva Rao. If I recall correctly, we approached the Defence Ministry who deputed an experienced accountant. He kept the accounts and I checked them daily. The day we made a hundred rupees was a great day! Can you imagine Rs. 100 in a day in 1948 ? It was incredible! I remember going on a holiday in the summer of 1948 and waiting anxiously for Prem or Kitty's postcards, reporting the daily sales figures!

Our first paid staff member was Teji Vir Singh, a war widow. My mother met her in the camp and persuaded us to engage this lovely girl. She stayed on for 30 years. The other salaried person was Mrs. Ahluwalia. These two ladies and the accountant were the only paid employees. The rest of us were all honorary workers.

As business increased, more and more women joined and we increased production. With the years, the refugee camps began to be dissolved but the group that worked on production continued.

Ques: How long did you continue with the Refugee Handicrafts and how did the transition to Cottage Emporium take place ?

Ans: In September 1949, I had to leave "Refugee Handicrafts" because my husband got posted to Washington. I handed over the honorary secretaryship officially to Prem Bery who worked there for many years to come.

In 1951, I received in Washington a cable from Kamaladevi Chattopadhyaya telling me about a proposal that the "Refugee Handicrafts" be taken over by the Indian Cooperative Union. I knew nothing about ICU. It came into my life only in connection with the "Refugee Handicrafts" and the "Emporium". I must say I was not very happy. "Refugee Handicrafts" was my baby — I had given birth to it! But I was in America and they were in India. So naturally I said all right. It was very kind of them to ask me. After all, I had no official hold on it. At the same time they also asked me to become a member of the All India Handicrafts Board under the chairmanship of Kamaladevi Chattopadhyaya, which I accepted with the greatest of pleasure.

On my visit to India in January 1952, the "Refugee Handicrafts" shop at Barakhamba Road shifted from the evacuee property to Janpath into the American barracks. These barracks were filthy, empty cells. One end of it — where later the gift centre was — was all burnt, the walls were smoky because the kitchen used to be located there.

That is how the "Refugee Handicrafts" shop came under ICU and was later merged with the "Central Cottage Industries Emporium." which was in the same building. With time it became a byword in the whole country. People came from all over India; foreigners visiting Delhi came to the "Emporium." State visitors were brought to the "Emporium." Had the "Emporium" kept a visitors' book it would have been a Who's Who not just of India but of the whole world. It became like the Taj Mahal — you had to see it! Except that from Delhi the Taj was far away but the "Emporium" was on

Janpath! Prem Bery would be there to receive the visitors and to show them round. They all went away fully satisfied, having purchased a lot.

Later on, very often when the President, the Vice President and the Prime Minister went on foreign tours, all the shopping for State presents of the Ministry of External Affairs was done at the "Emporium". It was a throbbing institution and the glory to everyone involved in it.

Ques: In what capacity did you work with the "Emporium" during this time ?

Ans: We returned to Delhi from Washington in 1954 and stayed till 1958. During those years I was a regular, non-paid worker at the "Emporium" — often taking visitors around, often travelling all over India on purchase missions. People often found me behind the counter selling. I remember the day when an American lady pointed to me and said in her American twang: "Didn't I see you in Washington? Isn't your husband the Ambassador?" I replied : "Yes, but I am working with this organisation because I love it." Whenever I came back to India or even during holidays, I worked there.

Ques: How long did your association continue ?

Ans: I resigned from the All India Handicrafts Board in September 1958 because we were sent out of the country again. I still remember the last day. With a bleeding heart I left my work I used to spend half of my time with the "Handicrafts Board" and half with the "Emporium". My life was that. On my husband's posting to Washington in 1958, I was appointed Chairman of the "Cottage Industries Export Committee of the Ministry of Commerce, Government of India". My counterpart in India was L.K. Jha, at that time Joint Secretary in the Ministry of Commerce. Kitty Shiva Rao was also in New York those days as her husband was with the United Nations. The two of us did bookings for export of Indian crafts. I recall carrying myself a suitcase full of samples to "Lord and Taylor" on the Fifth Avenue. Because of my husband's position, I got entry everywhere easily. With the help of God we were able to establish ourselves. Although L.K. Jha was our official counterpart in India I always turned to the "Emporium" to do the job and this is how exports picked up.

On my request the Vice President of "Macy's" came to India to visit the "Emporium". Thus, direct contact was established between "Macy's" and the "Cottage Industries". Similarly, "Lord and Taylor" sent their buyers to Delhi and "Nieman Marcus" did the same. Kamaladevi came to stay with us one year in Washington. We had to attend an Indian exhibition of crafts and textiles at "Nieman Marcus" in Dallas, Texas, with Kamaladevi as the chief guest.

It was a cooperative effort of women deeply concerned not only about refugee crafts but gradually all the crafts of India. Export expanded so much that by the time my husband relinquished his post in Washington in 1968, the government opened "Sona" in New York—a shop dealing in the crafts of India which was like an extension of the "Emporium".

On the last day of our stay in the United States the *New York Times* carried a long article reporting that the wife of the Indian Ambassador was behind the counter selling crafts of India in "Sona". I couldn't tear myself away from helping the craftspeople of our country and what better way than exporting their work. Unfortunately, "Sona" did not last too long.

Ques: Was the potential for the export of Indian handicrafts realised ?

Ans: Well, I recall how inadequately we were prepared for exports ! In the middle of the summer of 1961 there was an exhibition in Chicago called the "International Exhibition of Crafts". The government had asked Kitty Shiva Rao and me to be in charge of the Indian stall. They sent us crafts the like of which the United States had never seen before — among them birds made of buffalo horn in Kerala. Everyone wanted to buy the displayed items but being a government affair we were not permitted to sell. After the exhibition we had to repack everything and store it at the Embassy.

During the exhibition, a potential buyer came. He was interested in the purchase of one million pieces of horn birds for the Christmas season and wanted delivery by November. I immediately informed

L.K. Jha, adding that the buyer thought that being a bulk order he would be able to get the birds cheaper. There was no answer for six weeks. Jha was contacted again. His reply arrived well after Christmas, explaining that India could not supply one million birds because (a) it would take at least two years to produce this number and (b) the craftsmen say that, in fact, it would cost more because they get bored doing the same thing over and over again! This is a facet of the true Indian craftsmen and that was the end of the sale of one million horn birds.

Ques: On your return to India this time did you go back to the "Emporium" ? How long did your association with ICU last ?

Ans: No. After returning I never went back to the "Emporium" because we were posted outside Delhi.

When you ask me about ICU, for me ICU was Kamaladevi and Lakshmi Jain. Whenever there was any problem there was Kamaladevi and there was Lakshmi. Later, the government took over the management of the "Emporium." Slowly, the old workers left. By the time Prem Bery left, somehow the heart had gone out of the organisation. And now that it has shifted to this monstrous new building, I don't have the heart to visit there.

Ques: Why is that ?

Ans: I find the new group of sales girls haven't got the spirit that prevailed in those early years. Why that same spirit is not there today, I don't know. I presume because everyone is salaried—the idea is to have a job and keep a job. And if you are a confirmed government servant, you cannot even be dismissed.

In those days all those who joined were recommended by friends. I suppose each and everyone who worked then had someone who was a refugee and they knew their plight. Initially that was the motivation. Later on, they felt similar dedication to us, who managed it—that we must help the people. We used to direct, advise, guide them and we were always there to help out. That spirit, unfortunately, isn't there any more. Kamaladevi isn't there and none of us are there any longer.

❐ ❐ ❐

ELEVEN

"Working closely with the craftspersons, I realised how their entire family used to contribute in creating every item."

— *Teji Vir Singh*

Ques: Where did you spend your early years ?

Ans: My family—my grandfather and father—belonged to Amritsar, but they hardly stayed there. I was born in Lahore and I studied there too. I didn't have much education, but I studied up to Intermediate. Then I got married to an army officer. Unfortunately, I lost my husband in the war and became a young widow. Those were terrible years for me. But some of my very close friends persuaded me to take up a job to help refugee women earn a living and face their difficult life and situation. When I did that, I realised that I was not the only one to have suffered.

Ques: When exactly did you begin work with the Cottage Industries Emporium ?

Ans: Around 1950, the Cottage Industries was started by the Government of India. At that time we were running the refugee handicrafts shop where we used to sell only some embroidered goods and some tailored clothes made by the refugee women. When Cottage Industries was opened by the government, they wanted to sell handicrafts from all over the country.

But it was a deadly place! You know what government offices are like—someone would go and bring half-a-dozen pieces here, half-a-dozen there and put them together in the shop. There was no effort made at anything. If some customer came and bought anything, that was fine. However, when they saw the work done in the refugee handicrafts shop which we did, that is, Fori Nehru, Mrs. John Mathai, who was the lady in charge, Prem Bery and myself, then the government decided to hand over the Cottage Industries to this organisation. That is when I was asked to take it over.

Ques: Can you recall some of the work that this job entailed ?

Ans: When I took over, it was extensive work. Piece by piece everything was counted, lists were made, some other girls were employed, for instance, Gulshan Nanda was the first one to be brought in to help me with the lists. We made huge lists of those items taken over from the government and also of those that we had brought.

Then, Mrs. Mathai felt that we should not be merely sitting in Delhi. She said : "You let this be run by the paid workers here—the accountant, salespersons, etc. You people should travel all over the country and bring what is saleable to Delhi." And that is exactly what we began doing.

Ques: How did you go about selecting the items to be brought to Cottage ?

Ans: We, that is two or three of us girls, used to travel all over the country. We soon realised that in every area, lovely crafts were being made but there was no place for the craftsmen to sell them. The people we met were all very skilled craftspersons but they could not read or write. They made the items but they did not know where to sell them, and consequently, they had no money to buy more raw material to make more items. So we went to their rescue and we started to buy their crafts.

But government offices being what they are, it took a long time for us to make payments to the craftspersons. Even if it took one month it was too much time for them. I remember that people like me would fight with the accountant to get the craftsmen's payments sent in time so that they could buy more raw material and make more crafts. And then we would get out again to travel. India is so large that it was not easy to cover all the States; but it was very interesting work. At home we fussed about having our little luxuries but out there we didn't complain at all because we felt like one of them.

On one of our tours, I still remember, we had to sleep on the floor and one night I said to the two girls who were with me that I find it very difficult getting off the floor in the morning. They suggested that I should sleep on the dining table, and so I started sleeping on the table!

In those days, these places we visited did not even have good hotels. We used to travel right from Kashmir to Kanyakumari, then come back to Delhi to organise things. We would find out what is selling what isn't, see where things need improvement, find out what the customer likes and dislikes and then go back on our tours again and guide the craftspersons about some slight change that they should make in the items so that they could have a better market. We were also suggesting new designs all the time.

Ques: Can you speak about the kind of atmosphere you had at work those days; a bit about your colleagues ?

Ans: To start with, the entire staff may have been about 100. Later, it increased. We consciously selected girls—like Gulshan Nanda, Preetam and Lata Vadhera, Maya Seth (later Johar)—who had the ability to pick up skills for spotting the customers' tastes and then make suggestions to the craftspersons for altering designs. Initially, we senior women would accompany them on their tours but then gradually they began going on their own.

As for the work itself, it was not just a service like the government service. It was a job which you really enjoyed doing. You dreamt of those craftswomen and men who used to sit on the floor and did not even have enough good clothes to wear. They had to wait till their wages were paid and then they could think of buying a blouse or a saree. So you empathised with them and automatically you wanted to help them. It was when we saw the conditions of these craftswomen with our own eyes that we would come back and urge the accountant to send their money order soon because often they did not have the money to even feed their children.

Ques: How did you feel about holding a job of such immense responsibility especially since you had never worked before ?

Ans: I grew with the job. You see, as the Emporium grew bigger and bigger, so did one's vision expand. Over the years, I came to know the areas of handicrafts in our country inside out. Working closely with the craftspersons, I realised how their entire families used to contribute in creating every one of the items.

I was a salaried worker. But the organisation had all those women who did honorary work and I don't have enough words to describe their commitment. Women like Fori Nehru, Prem Bery and others would come and devote their time to the work, then go out and travel. And of course, there was Kamaladevi Chattopadhyaya who was the mother of the whole place! Her word was our command. Whatever she said we would do. One of the things I remember about her is that she was never too tired for anything. If necessary, she would walk barefoot; if necessary she would go without anything to drink the whole day—she devoted her entire life to this work.

By the time I retired after 33 years of service, I was 60. About six years before that, the government had taken over the running of the Emporium again. It became very commercial, but since we—the older staff—knew the tricks of the trade, we managed to carry on at least for some more time.

❑ ❑ ❑

TWELVE

"At the Cottage, most of the sensitive jobs were done by women who worked with tremendous commitment."

— *Suman Benegal*

Ques: When and how did your interest in crafts begin and how did you get involved with the work ICU was doing ?

Ans: Although I was very young during our freedom movement, I was keenly interested in what was going on. My father was from the North West Frontier Province and my mother was from Lahore. They had moved out before the partition and had settled in Simla. But I did my education in Delhi.

I was always very keen on reading newspapers and talking to people. My elder sister, Snehalata Sanyal, who was far more involved in all this, was the one who really got us into this area of work. She would discuss things with all of us, make us read and get us interested in our art, culture, crafts, etc.

I came to know about ICU only in relationship to the crafts emporium that they used to run. After the partition, I finished my four years of college and then worked with an organisation that was set up by the government to help repatriate people to India and Pakistan.

At that time (sometime in 1956) I also helped a friend of mine who was organising an exhibition on crafts. This was when Fori Nehru met me and asked me if I would be interested in working in the area of crafts. I thought to myself, why not, and felt it would be a good idea. In any case, I was already familiar with the Cottage Industries Emporium that one used to visit. It was a very, very small set-up then. So I joined the Cottage and that's how I first came in contact with ICU.

In the Cottage we had a lot of women working. Most of the sensitive jobs were done by women. For instance, the buyers were all women. Some of the top jobs were with women like Kamaladevi Chattopadhyaya, Prem Bery, Teji Vir Singh. And they all worked with tremendous commitment.

I worked with the Cottage from 1956 to 1965. Then I joined the Handicrafts and Handloom Export Corporation where the accent was on export and where I handled the development of craft and design.

Ques: What was the work assigned to you at the Cottage ?

Ans: My sphere was related to merchandise and, specifically, selection of merchandise. I had to travel a lot, selecting crafts from different parts of the country. When I joined, a team was slowly built up and we began selective buying for the Cottage—not just taking things which people came and left on consignment basis. We began travelling around the country, identifying and picking up things of a particular quality and standard to give a unique base to the Cottage. Then we got people coming from abroad to advise us on how items could be departmentalised.

Ques: What are some of the lasting memories you have of your years at the Cottage ?

Ans: The commitment of the first batch that we had was tremendous to this field because this was something that was just taking shape and growing; it was not something that was already set. Today, when people look at the Cottage, it's all already there.

When you had people like Kamaladevi giving you the guidelines and when you saw for yourself what she was doing for craftspersons, naturally, you got inspired. It was not like it is today when everything is so commercial, when people look at your degrees and people hop from one job to another. People who came there to work for ICU in the Cottage were all so committed because they believed they were doing something special and also because it was something they were starting. That made all the difference.

There was a pride in doing things by hand; there was this whole pride about *khadi*. All these things combined to give you that push to be involved in this work. It was also one of the jobs that parents allowed their young daughters to be involved in. They felt they could take it up without any prejudice. When they heard about the work ICU was doing and the kind of people who were involved, they felt this was one place their daughters could go to.

Ques: Can you describe the process of work at the Cottage ?

Ans: We all had our ups and downs but we learnt the entire process because this kind of a thing had never been done before. We all had to look at things and judge the good from the bad. Not only did we have to learn to judge the quality, but the pricing too had to be done with the greatest attention to detail. These were skills that one developed on the job. Then, slowly, we started working out the details with the craftspersons—actually giving them the colours, the patterns, etc. That is when the designing aspect also came up.

We travelled extensively in groups to different areas, took notes and then went back to get the items. The craftspersons were all identified through contacts and then slowly when word got around about this place in Delhi that was looking for crafts, they started coming to us. When the Handicrafts Board was set up, they began listing people and that helped a lot.

Those days every State used to encourage craftspeople to have a cooperative so that one could go to them and give the boost needed by passing the middlemen. You couldn't go to individual craftspersons because it was not easy to do that, but it was easy to do so through the cooperatives.

ICU was the organisation that laid the basis for all these cooperatives. If it were not for them and the kind of people they had working with them, the Cottage would not have started the way it did. It is because of this solid foundation that even today, although there are many other places, people still look to the Cottage for handicrafts.

Over the years, ICU finally found that they needed more funds to give the Cottage a bigger boost and that is when they handed it over to the government, because then the government could give the grants.

Ques: Do you feel that if ICU had continued till today, things would have worked in the same manner ?

Ans: Well, the times now are so different from what they were then. The new generation thinks so differently. Those days it was like a family feeling which will never happen any more. The whole approach to work—whatever field you are in—has changed everywhere now. For one, the operations are so huge these days that it can never happen now.

Things change. Even if you have found a good base and a good system, that's not a guarantee for a lifetime and for centuries to come. Concepts that once worked are not applicable now. A look at history can teach us this. Values have totally changed now, there's just no question of that. We are aping the West. Of course, they are professional, but there's also this constant feeling that one must be always getting ahead. Things have become very competitive. So then what can the youngsters do today? I am not finding fault with the new generation. I too have two sons and I know how much stress there is for youngsters today.

But I think we need to remember that nothing lasts forever. And that there is never a perfect system. Things change, the world changes, people change and with that the whole atmosphere changes. ICU did an excellent thing. It left a good feeling with everyone and then it handed over, because otherwise, it would have become very difficult for them.

❐ ❐ ❐

THIRTEEN

"The meaning of the word 'success' was how much rehabilitation of crafts we could achieve; how many crafts we could prevent from dying out."

— *Una Hiremath*

Ques: Can you recall how you got interested in crafts and then your first association with ICU ?

Ans: I was 12 years old when we came to Delhi after the partition. I remember the Cottage as a refugee handicrafts shop and that interested me a lot because when we had just come from Pakistan and I was a child, they used to hold these sewing sessions at Lady Irwin College where they stitched winter clothes for the refugees. Delhi's ladies used to ask all the women to come and help. My sister was a college student then. I used to go there and see all these women like you and me doing this wonderful voluntary work. By the time I finished college I was definitely interested in this field.

When I got out of college, there weren't all that many avenues that young women now have We were the second or third generation of women after Independence, coming out of university and it was a pretty straightforward choice that women had—you became either a doctor, or teacher, or professor and that was it.

I had studied literature and was quite sure that I would become a teacher. But by the time I got around to deciding what I would like to do, Kapila Vatsyayan, who was one of my teachers and knew me in college, told me that Kamaladeviji and L.C. Jain were looking for young people who would be right in the field of crafts to work with them. So they sent for me. I went there and I can't tell you how scared I was. I was so overawed. Kamaladeviji sat in that big office and she asked me what I had done. I said I had done English Literature and she asked if I would like to work with them. I said I'd like to but I didn't know anything about all this. So she said they would teach me. I said how could I expect to be taught at their expense, and I didn't think I could really work there. I was so overawed that I just said I couldn't do it!

Then I met L.C. Jain and he asked me to at least come and see what they were doing. Reluctantly and still very apprehensive, I went and I met all these wonderful people that I had heard about. This was in late 1958 and they suggested that I should take a month there and just spend time in whichever department I wanted. Then, at the end of the month, I could decide where I wanted to be. At the end of that month I told them that the area that interested me most was textiles. So they handed me a basketful of swatches of cloth and a pair of scissors and asked me to make a swatch book and see the different kinds of fabrics, and learn what comes from where—a kind of catalogue. It was fascinating and I sat down and did that and for me it was a piece of art. It wasn't enough to just put swatches together, I would match colours, etc—it brought out a lot of things from my mind that I did not know existed.

After this they sent me as an observer member with their buying team, all over the centres where fabric was produced. I came back feeling so close not just to the fabric but also to the origins, because once you've seen the weavers, the kind of places they live and work in, your involvement is quite different. That, in a way, set the spirit in which the Cottage and ICU worked. They weren't asking for credentials of your work experience and what degree you held in this line—it was your interest, your attitude that mattered. You got so personally involved that the one thing you forgot to ask in all of this was: how much would they pay ! The commitment that came with this work stayed with you in all you did and that's how textiles and weavers became a life-long interest for me.

Ques: How was it working with the Cottage in those days ?

Ans: I think what brought this spirit into us and the craftspersons were the people who got these teams together. There was Kamaladeviji whose interests were so well known—she was a legend in her lifetime—there was Kitty Shiva Rao, there was Prem Bery. And it didn't matter that they were all big names. There was that spark of almost respect that flowed between the craftsmen and them, and also a keenness in passing on that interest to the younger generation. So they didn't dismiss us; we were treated as equals—something that no office does today. If I felt there was something I wanted to do, or I wanted to question something, or had an idea, I just had to knock and walk into L.C. Jain's room. He was the big boss but he would always find the time. Attitudes were different. I could go up to any of the seniors and they would respect me and give me the kind of attention that they gave each other. When I made a mistake, it was always: "Doesn't matter, how will you learn if you don't make mistakes?"

Ques: What do you remember as the strengths of ICU ?

Ans: Well, they made you feel as if you were part of the community. I think it was one of the main strengths of ICU that they instilled in us the concept that the meaning of the word "success" was how much rehabilitation of crafts we could achieve; how many crafts we could prevent from dying out. That is the kind of spirit that was transmitted to us by people in ICU. And we worked as a team achieving that. Today, success is measured by the scale of pay, the margin of profit, your equity worth, etc. These were not things one thought of then.

You had a definite bond that held you together; that was the strength. It was a great challenge because it was a time when everything British was what was right and fashionable. To bring in a revolution where you were not only changing the availability of what were consumer goods, but actually making a whole generation aware of this and wanting to buy Indian crafts while appreciating their beauty. What ICU made us aware of was that you were not great designers wanting to change the world—you were a bridge between the village and the city because the city needs had changed and our job was to make the village person aware of those changed needs, without, in any way, destroying his spirit or craft.

We sat at the feet of these craftsmen in villages and yet we carried a bit of the city with us to help them see the change and slowly change their mindset to more contemporary demands. But there was this bond between us and the craftsmen. Today, they dictate to the weaver what to do and what not to do, so in a way they use him and destroy his touch too. That was the big difference.

ICU also showed great respect for the potential of the young people who worked with them. Although they did not have huge sums of money, they spent on our travels, etc., for instance, if you travelled alone, you were always sent by air and put up in the best hotel possible. All these things made you feel special in this place and that's why all of us feel a sense of loss that it didn't continue.

Ques: What do you think were the reasons for ICU not continuing ?

Ans: I left the Cottage at the end of 1964 as soon as I realised that the government was taking over. I said enough is enough, that if I have to be a slave I might as well get married! In many ways the changes had started earlier. On hindsight, I think the total trust and commitment that was our strength—which meant responsibility been given at even a young age—I think there were a lot of people taken on who did not have the capacity to take up that kind of responsibility. They started demanding all kinds of formalities like seniority, etc. So that our strength at this point became part of our weakness.

However, ICU achieved a tremendous amount in those few years. Not only did we set up whole systems of communications between the city and villages through this medium, but there were several other enlightened measures—the first flower shop, the art gallery, the cafe, the music shop—all this was achieved. Maybe it was trying to do too much too soon. I think when you grow too fast you can't have hand-picked people, so you take in a lot of people who are looking for merely a job and for climbing up, and then the rat race starts. And the sense of equality gets damaged. You have to have a shared goal to become a community. If you get even a few people who are there for their ambitions, then the problems start. That is what happened to us.

Sometimes I feel there is a time for everything—there is a time for commitment, there is a time for other things. Cottage happened at a time when there was commitment. All of us were looking for something; India was still a place with a cause. As life began to settle, economic problems took over, population pressures took over, the attitude to commitment changed, the attitude to and measure of success changed. By the 1960s this was already happening, and in a way we (the earlier lot) were still working with the sense of commitment which the new lot were not bringing with them.

Maybe the change had to come; maybe it is a process of evolution where you did not want to be sharing in a movement but wanted to make something of yourself. Maybe the change would have come eventually, it would have evolved. With the government coming in it became a very drastic cut.

While we were still there as a community, you saw the changes happening and I may be biased, but my own feeling is that once it went to a different management, nobody went into the strengths of what the Cottage was or what ICU was trying to achieve with the Cottage. So this whole process of trying to involve your workers with the crafts movement stopped abruptly.

What's happening now, for instance, is that buyers are not going out to the craftsmen, the craftsmen come to sell. So you are not developing products any more, you are just choosing what you are shown. You look around you and say well red is the colour that is selling so the Cottage buys red. Whereas in the old days you went to the weaver, had a dialogue and were actually setting the trend. Now they are following the trend. Now when you walk into the Cottage it's just like any other store; it's no longer a shop that is evolving. In a way, it is the only shop in this area of focus which is large enough to absorb new ideas, but those new ideas are not there.

Ques: Has this shift in focus affected craftspersons ?

Ans: Yes, a couple of things have affected this. One is that the give-and-take is not there anymore—the relationship is between the buyer and the seller, not between people who are learning from each other. Secondly, as I understood, our role was that whatever happens the craftspeople must be paid immediately. When they send you their stuff they don't have the staying power because you were trying to cut out the middleman, so their bills must be paid. But the government took over and they don't pay. So they have pushed them back into the middleman's hands. Therefore, the craftsperson was lost. And no longer was the craftsman looking to them (the Cottage) for help.

To give you an example: Years later, I got a phone call from Kamaladeviji asking me to drive by her house. I went and there she was sitting with two cartons full of *irkal* sarees from Karnataka. She said that the weavers came in and said "Amma, we've got these sarees and no one is buying from us so we're leaving these with you, you get the money for us." She said she didn't know how to say no to them so she asked me to somehow, through my friends and contacts, try to sell these sarees. The next day, she said I had to send the weaver a cheque for Rs. 2,000. Now, in the old days this weaver would have gone to the Cottage. But he no longer felt he could do that. Instead, he came to Kamaladeviji who was an old lady by then, not connected with the Cottage any more. So these were the kind of bonds that the craftspersons had, which went missing from the Cottage. It leaves one with a great sense of loss and vacuum. And this has particularly affected the small weaver who has no staying power.

Ques: Can an organisation like ICU do well in today's situation ?

Ans: It's difficult to think of, but certainly, I feel there is a great need today for an organisation like ICU. In many ways "Dastakar" has tried to fulfil that need. To some extent the State Emporia have tried to do it but completely without imagination. Once in a while you get good people who head the Emporium, but those are only flashes in the pan. There is no concerted effort to get the right people in at the right time.

Today, I feel our crafts are back in the same position they once were—they need help, they need guidance and they need protection. We're dealing with commercial sharks today and I'm not sure our craftsmen are ready—or ever will be—to deal with these sharks. So there's a great need for a place like ICU's Cottage. I don't think there is a lack of committed people or committed clientele—I think what we lack in a very, very big way is the leadership. We had it then; unfortunately, we don't have it today.

❒ ❒ ❒

FOURTEEN

"Working with the craftspersons was both a teaching and a learning experience."

— *Uma Anand*

Ques: Can you recall when you first came in touch with ICU ?

Ans: Teji Vir Singh and Fori Nehru were family friends of mine and they were instrumental in taking me to Cottage Industries in 1958. It had a very nice atmosphere and they went all out to help people, especially those like me—I was a young widow then. Fori Nehru gave me a long lecture and told me that I must come out now, that I just can't sit at home. That was a big step for me as I had never worked earlier. It was the first time I was going out to work, so it was just the right atmosphere—absolutely like a family. Even when you made a mistake, you were certainly reprimanded but in such a nice manner! The atmosphere was very healthy and they were all very encouraging towards women getting out and working.

When I joined, N.N. Dutta of ICU was looking after the Cottage. I remember, one year on Diwali day, one of the craftsmen brought a gift for me. I got quite upset and took it to Dutta and told him what had happened. He made me sit down and explained to me that these things happen in business and it was all right, I should not worry about it. So it was the kind of atmosphere where you could go to your seniors with any problem, without any kind of hesitation. They were always very encouraging, very understanding and supportive.

All the people involved with ICU worked with such complete dedication. I really enjoyed working there, and perhaps that's why I worked there for 30 years. It gave me a chance to travel around India and also abroad. I wish it had always remained like that. It was sad to see the gradual evaporation of that atmosphere at the Cottage.

Ques: Do you attribute this change in the Cottage to ICU's moving out ?

Ans: Well, you see, ICU was a completely dedicated unit. After them the Cottage gradually became commercial. Attitudes slowly began changing but still those of us who had worked and trained with ICU continued to have a great regard for the craftspeople and their crafts.

The very aim of ICU starting the Cottage was to give work to craftspeople, to encourage Indian crafts. So it was a great joy to work with the craftspeople. Later on the attitude at the Cottage became one of: "Where will these craftsmen go? They will have to come here to us." ICU never had that kind of attitude. Their attitude was that the craftspeople have to be encouraged, their craft, which was till then so invisible, had to be developed.

Ques: What did your work at the Cottage involve ?

Ans: To begin with, I was trained in just the showroom. Then I was taken into the buying department where I continued for almost all my 30 years there. I loved working with the craftspeople. I had to travel a lot, go to the craftsmen in the villages. They were really poor. We spent a long time with them, we sat with them, told them what to do. Sometimes we had to help them monetarily too—which of course the Cottage did, and that was another aim of ICU, to help the craftspersons with funds by way of advance, etc.

As far as the crafts were concerned, we really had to work very hard to make them produce samples. I remember the time I first went to Khurja. It was a completely dead town then, with people making only sanitaryware, switches, etc. I asked them why they had switched over to this from pottery? One old man told me that he had five sons, but not one of them was interested in doing pottery. It was through ICU's training that I could convince him to try and get his family interested, teach them and revive this craft because we would buy it from them. One of the main aims of ICU, after all, was to revive dying crafts.

On my part, I enjoyed every aspect of the work, especially working with the craftspeople. I—as were many of us who had joined then—was new to the area of craft but we all learnt on the job and one learnt a lot from the craftsmen. It wasn't as if you were only teaching them, but you learnt from them too. When I joined, the Cottage was a very small outfit and it did not have too much by way of sales. We travelled all around, looking for new sources, new crafts, new craftspersons. For example, at that time Moradabad was making only small coasters and things like that. Gradually, after spending some time with them, you gave them some ideas, they gave you some ideas. Working with the craftsmen was both teaching and learning.

I was handling handicrafts; I never handled handlooms. Later I headed the handicraft department in the buying section. I had one daughter who was only six years old then. I had my sisters here and sometimes I would leave her with them when I had to travel. Of course, it was not a very happy situation but it had to be done and I must say that the child was also quite understanding. There were times, especially when I went to the South, when the tour sometimes lasted a month. At times I asked my mother to come over. Then gradually I was able to do these long tours during my daughter's summer vacation so that she could be sent to her grandmother's. And because of the wonderful atmosphere, I never considered her as my child—she was a Cottage child! She could go to anyone if she had a problem.

I remember once I had to go to Srinagar on some charity buying after the war when we were buying directly from the craftsmen. It was Diwali time and my daughter was in Delhi. Our stay in Srinagar was suddenly extended and Prem Bery sent a message saying: "Don't worry about your daughter, I'll take care of her during Diwali." Today, this kind of attitude is very difficult to find anywhere. Not even in the Cottage. It's still good but it has become more commercial. It's true everywhere, where people are doing their work as just a job, and money is what matters.

Ques: What were the kind of changes that came about when the government entered the scene at the Cottage ?

Ans: When ICU was managing the Cottage, we had full liberty to buy what we thought would sell. Nobody questioned us unless, of course, the items were really not up to the standard. Later, the government appointed all kinds of committees for the various tasks and some of us working there thought there was unnecessary criticism. For us, the Cottage was like our own; it was like our personal shop.

Ques: What were some of your memorable experiences there ?

Ans: One of the most rewarding experiences was when the craftspersons got national awards for the items with which we helped them. Of course, it was their work and their effort, but somewhere I think we too helped and guided them to produce those items. You felt very good when those craftspersons you had either discovered, or worked with got national awards—and a lot of them did. It was also so satisfying to see that through the efforts and help of the Cottage, the standard of living of many of the craftspersons improved, and this was one of the basic ICU aims.

There was this particular case of a craftsman from Orissa who did stone work. In a sense, we had discovered him and brought his work to the notice of the Cottage. He was seriously ill, on dialysis and in bed. But we persuaded him to enter one of his items—a Ganesh statue—in an exhibition and it won a national award. Not only this, subsequently he got free medical treatment for his problems.

So you see, that kind of work, which you knew was benefiting so many deserving and needy people, was very satisfying. ICU often helped these craftspersons with advances and loans to set up their kilns, etc. All this went towards encouraging their craft. Now people tend to work for themselves and I think that is the difference.

Ques: Do you feel that an organisation like ICU would work in today's scenario ?

Ans: I think people have changed today. That kind of involvement, dedication and commitment is rarely seen now. You see, we had just won our independence those days. The sheer idea of being independent after such a long time really encouraged us and we were very enthusiastic. ICU did great work at that time especially with refugees and by setting up cooperatives and at places like the Cottage. I personally feel we do need that kind of an organisation today, but how many people will come out and join such an organisation? That is a big question mark.

❑ ❑ ❑

SECTION III

FIFTEEN

"I have never been in favour of a voluntary organisation being supported by the government and foreign funding agencies."

— *Sitaram Goel*

Ques: Can you recall something about your childhood and the influences in your early life ?

Ans: I came from a very poor family. We used to live in a village in Haryana. My father lived in Calcutta but he was a total failure; he never made any money. He was a broker in the jute goods trade and then he took to speculation and never did anything. He was a good for nothing. My mother brought us up.

From class VII onwards, I studied in Delhi and stayed with my brother-in-law who was a teacher in the Mahavir Jain School. L.C. Jain was my boyhood friend and we were together in this school and then in Hindu College. He was, I think, two or three years my junior.

But what mattered more was that we had an intellectual group here — the Changers' Club. Those days a Marxist sentence was in fashion, which said: "Philosophers have only interpreted the world; the task, however, is to change it." Most of us were influenced by Marxist and the progressive thought in those days. So we came together and had a lot to do with each other around 1944-45.

During college I moved towards Marxism under the influence of most of the professors who were well known and supposed to be intellectuals. But when I myself read deeply later on, I realised that they were just fools. But you see this was the passing fashion then just as the secular print is today. I also came under that influence. I had not yet become a Communist but I was quite a Marxist. The leader of our intellectual group was our friend Ram Swarup, who was really the guiding light in my life.

I did my M.A. in 1944 (I got first class in both B.A. and M.A.). Then in late 1944 I had to leave Delhi and I settled in Calcutta for 12 years. But I came to Delhi quite frequently. It was in 1949 that

Ram Swarup came to Calcutta and he knocked me out of Communism. He said: "You've done a lot of work for Communism, now do some work for Democracy also."

At that time, Lakshmi (Jain) was working at Faridabad as the assistant administrator under Sudhir Ghosh, and whenever he heard that I was in town he would get in touch and we would all meet at the United Coffee House. Sometimes all the friends would get together—Prof. Raj Krishna who was also my class fellow, Dr. Daya Krishan who became the vice chancellor and some other friends—and it used to be a great meeting!

But one occasion I remember very well. I was staying with Lakshmi at that time at Tilak Marg which was called Hardinge Avenue in those days. He was staying in the *kothi* of B.N. Rau, the Constitutional Adviser. I stayed with him for quite a few days, exchanging notes and so on. Then one day he invited me to visit Chhattarpur where ICU was working on one of their many projects. Lady Mountbatten was to visit that place. I saw her from very close quarters and was amazed to see really how democratic she was, at least outwardly.

As she stood there, practically all the people from around the village came to talk to her. But one man, a sweeper, with his broom under his arm, stood aloof and just went on looking. Lady Mountbatten noticed this and asked why he didn't come to meet her and wondered if she should go to meet him. The people who were around her—mostly Punjabi refugees—said, "Oh he's just a local". You see, even then, "refugee" had become a prestigious word and "local" was tainted!

Ques: What were your activities in Calcutta ? Did you continue with Communism ?

Ans: In 1948, I was a rabid Communist when the second Party Congress was held in Calcutta where they declared war on the Indian Republic and so on. Around that time, Ram Swarup had become an anti-Communist and we argued for months and months together where I would use slogans and he would use facts and arguments.

Ultimately, he made me read certain documented studies about Communism which changed me and I had to rethink the whole social philosophy. In 1949, I became an anti-Communist and I started writing letters against Communism mostly in *The Statesman* in those days—in fact, I became famous for writing these letters.

In 1952, we started an organisation called "Society for the Defence of Freedom in Asia" for informing our people in India about the danger which Communism poses. For instance, I wrote about seven studies on China and translated some books like *The God That Failed* into Hindi and thus, our work went on.

You see, we had started on the assumption that Pandit Nehru was a nationalist and democrat but . . .

Ques: What makes you say that ?

Ans: Well, there were plenty of instances but I'll tell you about one. I had written a book *Conquest of China* which was dedicated to Chiang Kai Shek—he was a great leader and he stood by India in 1942 against the British. He wrote a personal letter inviting me to visit Taiwan. There were no diplomatic relations between Taiwan and India, so I did not know what the passport situation was. I sent my whole correspondence with Chiang Kai Shek to the Ministry of External Affairs and sought their advice about whether I should accept this invitation.

There was no reply for several months and I applied for a passport in Calcutta. After a few weeks, the deputy secretary asked me not to bother him because my case was not with him—in fact, he told me that it was not in Calcutta but in Delhi, and with someone very high up. I understood that it was with Pandit Nehru. Some Congressmen assured me that Nehru was a democrat and everybody got a passport. They advised me to write a personal letter to Pandit Nehru which I did. But he wrote back (I still have that letter), and without any explanation said that passport facilities could not be granted to me. In later years too I was not given a passport. The first passport I got was in 1977 when the Janata Party came to power and Lakshmi got it for me.

Ques: How long did your Society in Calcutta carry on ?

Ans: By December, 1955 we had to close down our Society in Calcutta. The government was after us, threatening to raid the place. I was finally sued, of all things, for obscenity! You can't, after all, work against your own government.

When Khrushchev was to visit Calcutta, they started coming to our office and demanding to know what we were going to do. We told them that after all, we were only writers trying to inform the people; we were not in the streets demonstrating. But they made things very difficult. There were always at least two dozen CID people all around me. Finally, the chief of the Intelligence Bureau rang me up and told me off the record that unless I left Calcutta before Khrushchev arrived, he would be forced to put me in preventive custody. I was not interested in going to jail so I left for Delhi, accompanied by my CID men, who handed me over to their colleagues in Delhi!

Ques: What did you do in Delhi ? Was this the time that you worked with ICU ?

Ans: I had been a very well placed executive in the jute export business which I had given up—I had given up my business career. Then Minoo Masani invited me and said they would finance me if I stood for Parliament (this was when the Swatantra Party idea was in the air). So the Jana Sangh gave me a ticket and the PSP also promised support and in the 1956-57 second general elections, I stood from Khajuraho. Well, I lost, and after that I stayed with Prof. Raj Krishna who was a close friend.

I told him that I was on the streets and nobody would give me a job in India. You see, I had applied for a job with the Birlas and instead of a straight letter refusing me a job, G.D. Birla had replied with a taunt saying: "There is no job in our house equal to your qualifications." Raj Krishna said that he would speak to Lakshmi, although, of course, the salary they would offer would be small. By that time Calcutta had become very hot for me, particularly my own community. The Marwaris hated me for working against Communism—they were the greatest friends of Communism. And then in 1969 during the Naxalite wave, when they had to run away

from Calcutta, they came to me. I said I am very happy; you should be destroyed.

Therefore, I was quite eager to be in Delhi. Raj Krishna talked to Lakshmi who said : "I welcome you here and I'll give you the highest salary possible." He also said that I should join but on one condition: No politics! I agreed and in April, 1957, I joined ICU.

Ques: How did you like working with the organisation ?

Ans: Well, you see, there were problems immediately. There was this Cooperative League of USA helping ICU's rural development department. Thomas Keehn headed the League's office in India. He took a great objection to me although I did not know him at all.

One day I was sitting with Som Benegal, who has always been a Stalinist (but I don't take him seriously, he doesn't take me seriously!)—we were joking and chatting. That day, McCarthy had died. Now I had never liked McCarthy, but Som jokingly said: "Oh, your great friend has died, you must be a very sad man today." So I too jokingly said: "Yes, a great man has died."

Just then Keehn walked in, overheard this and said I must be a very bad man to feel this way about McCarthy. I said to him: "Mr. Keehn, we have not even been introduced and you have no business to call me names."

I had with me an article I had written saying that it is America which is selling this red poison called dialectical materialism to the whole world. So I handed Keehn this article. He read it and just flared up. His house, like every American's house those days, was a hotbed of Communism—you could meet every Communist in town there. Because then Communists were respectable people and Americans always go with respectable people. Anyway, he just walked away in a huff.

A few months later I came to know from some other sources that very evening Lakshmi and Som were both invited to Keehn's home for dinner. When they got there Keehn was lying in bed. Lakshmi asked him if he was ill. And all the Americans came up and said that this Communist reporter from Calcutta had insulted Keehn.

Lakshmi knew that I had a very sharp tongue and felt that I may have said something so he explained to Keehn that my reputation, in fact, was one of being an American agent in this country! Then Som, the beautiful corrector, explained the situation to Lakshmi and said that if anyone insulted anyone it was Keehn who had insulted Sitaram. So Lakshmi said to Keehn: "I give you 24 hours; you can fold up your aid programme and leave ICU if you wish, but I will not be dictated to about who I keep in my organisation." After that the Americans were on their knees.

The next day, Keehn came and we shook hands and we became friends also. But Lakshmi had to face many other people like Keehn because of me, because the atmosphere was full of Nehruism before Mao Tse-tung burst his balloon in 1959.

Ques: What was the kind of work you did with ICU ?

Ans: During my two years in the research department of ICU I did a lot of work. And all this work was recognised by Lakshmi and everybody else. Particularly, the work I did in the critical review of the Reserve Bank of India's Rural Credit Survey. I dug up the whole bunch of lies they had been telling everybody. They had never discussed this and yet they said it had been fully discussed in the country.

Then there was my experience with the Panchayat Parishad. There were two organisations started by Balwantrai Mehta—the All India Panchayat Parishad and Council for Africa. He had chaired the Committee which made the famous Panchayati Raj Report. He was trying to coordinate Panchayat work. Later on when he went into politics, he handed over the Panchayat Parishad to Jayaprakash Narayan.

When JP took it over he found that the organisation didn't even have a constitution, so how could it ask for aid from the government. He began looking for someone who could put the Panchayat Parishad on its feet. He asked Lakshmi who said: "I can give you a man but you don't like him and he doesn't like you."

JP said: "I can understand me not liking somebody but who is there who doesn't like me." So when Lakshmi mentioned my name, his first reaction was: "*Bahut bhayankar aadmi hai!*" ("He is a terrible person.") But he agreed to meet me.

I went to meet JP and we exchanged a few words about the shape of things in India. He liked what I said and he took me on. He asked me to frame a constitution for the Panchayat Parishad in one week. I did this and gave it to him. That very evening he phoned to say that he had shown it to the Law Ministry and they couldn't find any fault with it. So the Panchayat Parishad started and it got a lot of money.

But suddenly one day JP sprung a surprise. A Panchayat Raj training institution was to be set up under the All India Panchayat Parishad. Lakshmi had me in mind as the Director for this institution, since I had worked for the Panchayat Parishad. Although JP had a good opinion about me, one fine day he just announced that he had found a director and he said to me: "But Sitaramji, he is a Muslim." So I told him that I too had Muslim friends, so where was the problem.

JP was a very fine gentleman, but he would listen to anything anyone told him. He lived very much in terms of public opinion. So he took this man as Director who immediately started trying to throw me out. My friend Dharampal also ganged up with him because he himself was interested in becoming the Director. So they got together to throw me out.

I could see their game as they tried to create problems between me and the Director. Then JP called a meeting between me and the Director to force a showdown, but it didn't work. So JP called for another meeting to which he also called Lakshmi, wanting to sort things out. When JP started talking about the problems, Lakshmi took me by the hand and said, "Let's go." JP wanted to know what happened. Lakshmi said to him: "Look, I had loaned him to you to put the Panchayat Parishad on its feet. Now it's functioning and there is no shortage of work for him. He's not to be at anybody's mercy." And he just dragged me out. So that is Lakshmi. The man with the biggest heart that I have ever met.

Then I worked with ICU again. But for two years Lakshmi had to face many people who were criticising me. I happen to be a man with a sharp tongue. Sometimes some Communist would provoke me and I would say something that would be reported to Kamaladevi. Then Lakshmi would become unhappy with me. I realised his position but sometimes I would lose control.

Those two years were very bad. Then towards the end of 1959 the Chinese trouble started and in the meantime, Lakshmi had also been to the Soviet Union. When he came back he held a meeting in ICU and there he described the kind of misery he saw with his own eyes in the Soviet Union. As people walked out of this meeting, they commented to me: "Mr. Goel, he's in your pocket now". I said to them that he had his own mind, and that I had not even talked to him after his return!

With the Chinese trouble, Nehru's stock started sliding. Then people started coming to me and saying that what I had said was correct. So my situation improved a lot. Then I started writing a series on Pandit Nehru which was published in the RSS paper, *Organiser*. (Even today, no other paper will publish anything I write. Today, Communism has collapsed, but the bad reputation I earned in those days is still haunting me.) The series was called "In Defence of Comrade Krishna Menon". It ran into many articles—about 17-18. Lakshmi did not know; he didn't have the faintest idea, as I was writing under a pseudonym.

At the end of 1963, I published those articles in the form of a book. But I did not know that the gang that had brought about all this tragedy was still in power, although they had lost face. One day, Ram Swarup told me that because of this book of mine, Lakshmi was in trouble. So I went to him and asked if this was true. Lakshmi looked at me and became furious. He said: "Sita, there are Communists in our organisation, there are Jana Sanghis, Socialists, everybody is free to say what he wants to say. I have not bought up their minds; they work in the organisation and I cannot be held responsible for what they write or what they say. Why is it that they make all this trouble when you write about something you feel intensely about? You are free to write. It's a democratic country. I'm not going to yield."

However, I realised that there was a lot of pressure on him. I told him that he had given me protection when I was on the streets and that is why I survived. But I had survived in the past and this time also I hoped to survive.

I said to Lakshmi that if he retained his position, then after some days he could again help me. But if he lost his position, then who would help me? So I called his steno Badrinath, and I dictated a letter saying: "Your services are terminated with immediate effect, etc." Lakshmi said: "Look, I'm not sacking you, you are resigning." I said to him that if I resigned, I would get only one month's salary; if I was sacked, I would get three months, salary! I had absolutely no honour left in this country! There were tears in Lakshmi's eyes that day.

But later, Lakshmi gave me another fellowship to carry out another survey which I could not do. He tried his best to help in whatever way he could.

There have been three people in my life who have helped me to stand up on my feet: my brother-in-law who educated me and kept me in his house; Lakshmi who picked me up from the streets; and a cousin of mine in Calcutta who helped me in my business.

Ques: Can you talk a little bit about the atmosphere at ICU's research department ?

Ans: Well, there was absolutely no intellectual atmosphere or research there. When I got there, Raj Krishna had moved out already—there were just three or four people. I was there, Ranjit Gupta was there and there were G.P. Srivastav, Devaki and one Capt. H.S. Lather.

The only serious intellectual work that was done, I think, was this report on joint farming which appeared under the names of Raj Krishna, L.C. Jain and Gopi Krishan. It had been written before I joined. This was a very serious piece of work and so was a report on Marketing of Handicrafts done by Raj Krishna.

To be quite frank, for me it was a kind of *agyatvasa* a refuge. I did whatever work was given to me and my work was liked and appreciated. But quite honestly, my heart was not in it. I have never been for these semi-government organisations because of their bureaucratic ways.

Take the case of the whole scheme of the Super Bazar. It was prepared in the ICU research department. When it was all finalised, and when ultimately Indira Gandhi asked Lakshmi to implement it in order to arrest the price rise, Lakshmi came with a great sense of triumph and said: "Sita, I'm going to make you the business manager." At that time I said something I should not have said and I have regretted it later on. I said: "Lakshmi, Socialism has been a failure with all this ideological effort having been made to prop it up. It seems that now it's going to succeed on the strength of personal ambition." Now, attributing personal ambition to Lakshmi was in very bad taste but somehow I blurted it. I was sorry for saying it. But then the Super Bazar turned out to be a disaster. Today, they are even selling medical supplies at inflated prices.

I did become chairman of the Super Bazar's book and stationery department and can still remember the amount of pilferage that went on. At that time Lakshmi was in a hurry to stock up, so most of the time, no inventory was taken of things that were bought.

Ques: But can you simply club ICU with all other organisations ? Was there nothing that made it stand out, in your opinion ?

Ans: I have not been in favour of these voluntary agencies supported by the government and most of them are also supported by foreign funding agencies which are working for either intelligence agencies, or State, or defence departments. I feel most of this voluntary effort has been pretty much of a hoax. But I must say, ICU did great work because behind it there was no careerism—so far as Lakshmi and some of the other people like Gopiji, Som Benegal were concerned —these people were never careerists. They really wanted to do something. In Faridabad, for instance, although the cooperative experiments there failed—the rehabilitation of the refugees was simply great work done by ICU, like which there is no other example.

Then the sort of work they did in the villages was very good —they were really out there to help. And the greatest work they did was in the field of handicrafts. Before ICU took charge of the Cottage, Indian handicrafts were practically unknown. I did a survey of All India Handicrafts Associations and there I found that the tempo of marketing had gone far ahead of the tempo of production. This problem was there but they did their best. They made a mark in this field and this was to the credit of the ICU team. The brain behind it was Lakshmi and some others. However, what I count more, is not so much the work done but the spirit behind the work. Of course, the entire Nehruvian model of voluntary work and State sponsored organisations has been a tragic failure. All this corruption that is being dug up today is the outcome of Socialism—everywhere, Socialism has been the most corrupt system, because if you give power to the baby, he will not stop at anything.

So organisations like ICU, I think, can just not work. I'll give you one instance. In my report on the association of workers and merchants and exporters in the field of handicrafts, the central recommendation was that over a period, the All India Handicrafts Board must be wound up and the work should be given to a voluntary organisation consisting of these handicraft workers, exporters, merchants and so on. What happened was that another deputy directorship was created in the handicrafts department for implementing this report! And nothing more came of it.

According to me, any government has only two jobs: one is to defend the country and the other is to maintain law and order. This, our government has totally failed in doing.

We should not forget that whatever success was achieved by ICU was more due to the type of people who supported it. If there was anybody else in Lakshmi's place, he would have minted money out of it. But this man walked out of it penniless.

Ques: How did you manage after you left ICU ?

Ans: I survived and later on started a business in the export of Indian publications, and built a house and today I'm a multi-millionaire. I retired in 1982, handing over everything to my sons.

From 1963-77 I was just busy building my business because under Indira Gandhi politics was also going downhill. However, in 1977 when Emergency was imposed, Ram Swarup, Lakshmi and I came together again and wrote a letter addressed to the Members of Parliament to come out against this. Nothing came out of it, because nothing could come out of such small efforts. But at least the fight was there.

As soon as elections were announced, Chandra Shekhar walked into Lakshmi's office, saying : "We have just come out of jail and we have nothing so could you get together some set-up to prepare for our press briefing, etc." So Lakshmi got together a group which also had Arun Shourie, Raj Krishna, Ram Swarup, Dinanath Mishra of the RSS, George Verghese, myself and a couple of others. What we did was to read the papers through the day and prepare some kind of brief comments which we would give them every evening. We were all very enthusiastic about the Janata Party.

One evening Lakshmi called me to see a pledge he had drafted which the Janata MPs were to take at Gandhiji's *samadhi*, that they would not quarrel among themselves, etc. So I told him this is very good but all these people were *puraney paapi* (veteran sinners!) And this turned out to be true—as soon as they came back from Raj Ghat, the fights started.

In 1981, I told Ram Swarup, "Look I am now 60 years old. I have married off my children and fulfilled all my duties to my family; now I have no more debts, except *rishi rin*."

❐ ❐ ❐

SIXTEEN

"Everyone who came in touch with us became very influenced by the ICU philosophy."

— *Bharat Sahai*

Ques: When were you born and how did you spend your early years ?

Ans: I was born on June 6, 1922, in Bihar. I moved to Benaras in 1940, completed my Matriculation and then got admission for Intermediate. I did Intermediate from Benaras Hindu University and then went on to finish my graduation. In 1942, I was fortunate to be among a group of friends who were, perhaps, more enlightened than I. We used to have regular meetings around our political and social activities, and to an extent around our educational activities. Basically, almost all of us were prepared to participate in the freedom movement when it started. And that is exactly what happened. The movement started on 9th August. Some of us dropped out of it, but others stuck on and had the privilege of being a part of it.

I still remember the day when an important meeting was to take place. Our Vice Chancellor, Dr. Radhakrishnan, was trying to persuade us not to leave the campus. But nobody listened to him because the predominant feelings in everybody's mind was that this was the last phase of our fight. As Gandhiji used to say, this was our last fight for Independence. Each one of us believed in that and we participated fully. We began our march from the University and when we got to Benaras Chowk where the *kotwali* was situated, the police opened fire to disperse the crowd. I was hit on one leg and was taken to hospital. Later, I was told that the march was very successful. They went up to the Court and from there at 6 o'clock in the evening, they all dispersed.

This was the beginning of my life in politics. My political activities continued and around mid-October I was arrested from my classroom and imprisoned in Benaras. After three years, in October 1945, I was released. Luckily, I had very good friends in jail who advised me to continue my studies and complete my B.Sc. examination before I started doing anything else. But I had no money and I was determined not to take any money from my father. So some friends sent me some money and I also started teaching a friend from my own class. This is how the 5-6 months passed and I appeared for the examination.

Ques: How did your political life progress ?

Ans: In the meantime I came in contact with Sucheta Kripalani's elder brother, Dhirenbhai, whom I had known even before going to jail. He asked me what I intended to do. I told him that I had no plans but I was certainly not going back home. He asked me to wait for his call and maybe something could be done. When I went home to see my ailing father I got a telegram from Dhirenbhai saying, "Come, needed in Delhi". So I went to the Benaras Gandhi Ashram where a ticket was waiting for me to go to Delhi. When I reached Delhi I was taken to Gandhiji for his blessings and from there I went to Meerut for the Congress session. I was assigned the duty of enrolling all those who took a stall in the exhibition ground. The Congress session finished and at the end of the session, Acharya Kripalani, who was the President, said that his wife who had just returned from Noakhali required more workers to go with her. So I ran to Dhirenbhai and told him about this. Till then, I did not know that Dhirenbhai was Sucheta Kripalani's elder brother. He advised me not be in a hurry. In the meantime he had spoken to Sucheta Kripalani and I was called to meet them in the Meerut Gandhi Ashram. Sucheta Kripalani asked me, if I was willing to go to Noakhali with her and I agreed readily.

So another chapter of my life started. I went with her to Noakhali and spent about two years doing relief work. Gandhiji had distributed the whole area in Noakhali to individual leaders, those who had gone to work there. Sucheta Kripalani was one of them. The area which was given to Sucheta Kripalani was ultimately assigned to all the workers working with her. After two years, Sucheta Kripalani was required to go to Delhi. She used to visit that city quite often but now she had to be stationed there because riots had started in Lahore and refugees began pouring into Delhi and the nearby places.

Ques: When did you first come in contact with ICU ?

Ans: The Congress had set up a committee called the Central Relief Committee (CRC). We all started working with this Committee. That was my first contact with the Delhi people; and then I came in touch with L.C. Jain who was one of the Camp Commandants on behalf of the CRC. The work in the refugee camps developed, and developed so tremendously that nobody thought of eating, nobody thought of sleeping. Entire days and nights the workers wanted to do something. People like me and many of my friends who never looked back were fully engrossed in this. Three to four years passed in this manner. Then came Independence. I was here in Delhi in the Parliament when the transfer of power took place. I stayed in Delhi with Sucheta Kripalani. There were opportunities for me to go to Bihar and other places to work also. But I decided to be with her.

Ques: When exactly did you join ICU ?

Ans: When I got married and further settled in life here, I got the opportunity to join ICU in 1952. I remained with it till November, 1955 as the Administrative Secretary and I found that it was a great training for me.

Ques: What was the kind of work involved ?

Ans: We organised different types of workers such as iron and steel workers. The Cottage Industries Emporium also came under us at that time. My experience in helping the Cottage Industries Emporium select people for the Emporium, arrange such workers who could be useful for us, it was all a wonderful training for me. I must say that the role played by ICU at that time, either individually or organisationally in different fields, was tremendous. I could see that there were a large number of boys and girls who came in touch with us and were greatly influenced by the ICU philosophy.

Ques: Why did you stop working with ICU ?

Ans: In 1955, I left ICU because I got an interview call from the Ministry of Rehabilitation. They needed my services. Thanks to my ICU experience in dealing with refugees, settling them, marketing the goods for them, arranging small work centres, etc., I got the opportunity of going to the UN. This was for management training and training in administration for social welfare services. When I returned from the UN after 9-10 months, I went back to the Ministry of Rehabilitation. That too was a great experience and opportunity because by then the Ministry had started arranging the dispersal of refugees who came from East Bengal and had gathered at Calcutta station.

I had a very good experience. The Ministry gave me certain responsibilities, to represent them and discuss with different States matters regarding the settling of refugees. After three years I was interviewed and selected for the post of Deputy Director of Exhibition. At this point I came to the All India Handicrafts Board. By then, L.C. Jain had become the Member-Secretary. I worked for 3-4 years and then I got the opportunity to appear again in the UPSC for a much higher position — that of a Director. I was selected. I became the Director and five years later I was selected for the post of Commissioner.

Ques: Which was your most memorable experience ?

Ans: The period as Director of Handicrafts was a very good experience. It was a position from where I could influence many craftsmen in terms of getting them different types of work, channelising their products for sale, getting them assistance from the state government. Until I retired as Commissioner, I was dealing with that scheme. Then came a very glorious time in my life. I was selected for the Development Commissioner's post but something happened and I was not allowed to join because I was not from the IAS or any such service. However, my work gave me enough strength to get back the position of Development Commissioner, carpet scheme. At that time the carpet trade alone was worth about Rs. 900 crores but India was not poised to capture the total supply. The Government of India thought of running a scheme in which the maximum carpet export trade could be captured by India. I was given the opportunity to run that scheme. I remember, the Prime Minister, Indira Gandhi, called a meeting in January to which I was also invited. When everything was being decided, I was given that responsibility. Thereafter, I was given the post of Development Commissioner also. I was there for five years and then I retired.

However, after that too, Indira Gandhi did not release me. She called me to help the government in an organisation — or, rather a department — which was set up and called the High Power Panel for Minorities, Scheduled Castes and Scheduled Tribes. I was the technical director there at that time. All the data that was prepared had to be checked. It started in 1980 and went on up to 1982. Then, I finally left the government and now I am with the Lok Kalyan Samiti. Here too, there have been groups which have been organising cooperatives. My contribution has been to ensure that all the workers are put on a regular pay scale and are given adequate help.

Ques: In what way did your association with ICU impact your life the most ?

Ans: Well, I must say that working together with others at ICU made me more disciplined. That training had an impact on me to do things correctly, to do them in time and not to embarrass people or become biased.

Ques: What do you feel ICU achieved in terms of its original aims and where has it come now ?

Ans: I do not know whether I am in a position to judge it in that way. But I saw that those who left ICU were able to successfully set up their own organisations.

I will say that discipline is one thing which we must emphasise. I remember ICU asked me to organise the Kalyani congress — ICU had been given the responsibility by the Congress to put up a full-fledged exhibition of handicrafts. I went to Calcutta where I stayed for nearly a month and a half, doing that work. It was a very hard time for me. I used to be in the *pandal* from 8 in the morning till 2 the next morning. I did it and I did it only because my heart and soul were with the movement. I thought if I fail here, ICU will be affected. They had selected me as the person to come and organise this. If I failed in that mission, well, I would be harming ICU . So this is the lesson that I got; this is the lesson that I conveyed to many of my friends.

Ques: What about the whole objective, the purpose with which ICU was formulated to provide opportunities for the small-scale sector and make it a pillar of the economy ? To what extent do you think this was achieved ?

Ans: I can say with pride that it fulfilled this objective 100 per cent. I can write pages after pages on my carpet industry where I had the opportunity of setting up a centre. Then I had the opportunity of training 50 boys in the centre and putting those 50 to work again. I can say, none of those boys are starving today. They have all flourished. And all this I could manage to do because I had received invaluable guidance and training from ICU which I can never forget.

❑ ❑ ❑

SEVENTEEN

" ICU was unique because it was reconstructing India, and because it was teaching people from Nehru downwards that you can reconstruct with the people."

— *Devaki Jain*

Ques: Can we begin at the beginning, with your childhood and early years ?

Ans: I belong to the old Mysore State—what used to be called the princely State of Mysore—which became Karnataka after the Independence. I was born in Mysore city, the capital of the old Mysore State. Much of my education, up to B.A., was broadly there but not always there because my father was a civil servant of the Mysore Civil Services which was almost a clone of the ICS.

My father came from the educated middle class ; from just an ordinary family. His father was an engineer, grandfather was a temple water-carrier. You know, the typical Brahmin background. My mother was the daughter of the manager of the Tirupati temple whose parents were all temple water-carriers (*pujaris*). One or two ancestors were Sanskrit *vidvans* (scholars) on both sides and one or two were ayurvedic *acharyas*. So it was that kind of a background; not a background of feudal owners of property like many Brahmins of the South have been. This was a straightforward family evolution from *acharyas* to engineers to civil servants.

Ques: Was there a great stress on education ?

Ans: There was and there was not. In the sense that my father was a brilliant man but although his mind was very radical, I think the pressures basically were to educate boys and not girls. Not wilfully, but I think it was an aura. So there was no particular interest in my education.

Except for a short interlude in the Hindi land, when my father resigned and became the Dewan of the Raja of Gwalior (Rajmata's husband), the rest of my education was in the South. College in Mysore and two years when I didn't study due to traditional reasons.

I wanted to work after my graduation so, thanks to my father, I found a job in Bombay with Minoo Masani whom he knew. It was in a small organisation called Democratic Research Service. The assignment that Masani gave me was to write a book on alternative development of India. Interestingly, he called it *Democratic Alternative* and he wanted to show that there was an alternative between full-fledged socialism and free enterprise.

You know, Masani in those days was a hero because he had written this lovely book called *Our India*, a very exciting book for children. At the time I knew him, he was a very vibrant man. He had very little money so I was the only research assistant and I was 22 years then.

Ques: How did you first get to know of ICU ?

Ans: Masani wanted me to write about cooperative societies, especially agricultural cooperatives. At that time there was a great deal of debate about agricultural cooperatives. The Russians had cooperatives but that meant that the land was entirely owned by the State. So there was this Socialistic type of cooperative and there was the liberal cooperative. Then there was the Gandhian notion of cooperative and the PSP type. It was part of the book *Democratic Alternative* which actually got published and was presented in Patna to a huge conference over which JP (Jayaprakash Narayan) presided. And I was the principal presenter of this book at the age of 22. The book was like a planned document and we had sections like agriculture, industry, etc., and in each he had wanted me to show an alternative.

In the research for cooperatives, he asked me to write to the Indian Cooperative Union in Delhi. So I wrote and I got a reply from an American man, Tom Keehn, who was from the Cooperative League in the USA. They were providing technical support to ICU. He sent me some books which I used.

It was an interesting accident of fate that one fine day this Tom Keehn landed up in the office of the Democratic Research Service in Bombay, saying that he was curious to know about this office and this "M.A. Devaki" who wrote them a letter seeking information. They, being obviously lively advocacy people, wanted to hunt down those who had asked for information.

The interesting thing was that there was enough time and space with people in those days so that people pursued and found out who was trying to reach out. Today, we get so much mail and so many inquiries that nobody bothers. But in those days, in the flush of post-Independence, this still happened. So this American turned up at my door and said: "We wanted to know what you did with the material." Then he asked me what I planned to do after this. I told him that I was on contract for three months at Rs 300 a month, to write this book. He asked if I was looking for a job after that and I said I would love one. He said ICU, which had a rural development division, was looking for researchers, and that when I did look for a job, I should write to them.

As soon as I finished my work with Masani I wrote to them and they called me for an interview. I came to Delhi and was among the three men and three women chosen to work in what was called at that time, the rural development section of ICU.

Ques: What would you say set you on this path ? Were there, for instance, any early influences in terms of persons or even ideology ?

Ans: No, no ideology. Certainly, I was a very active member of the college student body, in the sense that I was secretary of the union, the secretary of every association—dancing, dramatic, etc. I'd say there was some kind of characterisation of natural leadership from then. Looking back, I find that, unfortunate as it is, it seems to come to some and not to others. I was a leader in college, I got three gold medals in college—I was a star performer in academics also. My degree was in Mathematics and English. I don't know how this happens. But if you look at other women I know in public life at some kind of well-known level, they've all had that peculiar track. I'd hate to claim I was different; it seems to be a genetic or god's gift. If at all I had an ideology, it was partly leadership; it was a desire to work. It's so difficult for your generation to understand, and I haven't been able to locate why is it that when I was 14-15, the one thing I said to myself was that I want to work. And yet there was nobody in the family—no cousin, no mother, no grandmother, no aunt, no sister-in-law—who had actually worked except inside the house. So I have no idea, from where you get that desire to work. But that was the driving force and after I did my B.A. I was restless till I got a job.

I also remember that from the age of five or six I seem to have got into a mode of caring. I would always be found either teaching someone, or taking out lice from the gardener's daughter's hair, or something like that. So perhaps caring for something outside oneself and care for independence—those could be the two pillars of ideology; but not necessarily public life, or freedom struggle. All those were too far away for us. We were a civil servant's children, we were very poor, we were locked into going to school and coming back, looking after our own clothes, our own food. My mother had no domestic help at all and she had the responsibility of looking after seven children, my father, her widowed mother-in-law, her widowed mother. Moreover, she had to look after different levels of brahmanical life. For instance, they would not eat if she had not bathed, etc.

I think my preoccupation with injustice and inequality must have been there somewhere. If you ask where I got it from, I think it was because my mother, her father, were humane people. My recollections of my mother are that she was always concerned about the pain of others. She had her own children but if anyone in the compound was having a baby she would cry till the baby was born —whether it was human, or of a cow, or dog. She was an amazingly sensitive person, so outside of self that I think demonstrably, she must have influenced our consciousness. She was extremely ethical, extremely concerned for the outside world and she influenced all of us greatly.

Ques: Did the excitement of the freedom movement touch you at all ?

Ans: No, it didn't touch us. It's very curious and I am myself shocked and ashamed. I once asked my brothers what happened and they said I was very young, and life at that time was very segregated for men and women even though we were not in a *purdah* area. Our lives were so domesticated. For instance, we could never go to watch a film or to a friend's house. When we came back from school, we stayed. There was no question of going out of the compound and if we wanted to go we needed an escort. So we were literally latched on to our mother's saree. Wherever she went we went with her.

There was no TV in those days to bring news into our house; the newspapers were probably in our father's room and never read by any of us. Looking back, my parents seemed to have had a lot more interaction with the freedom struggle. They had met Mahatma Gandhi, my father had protested against the white men subordinating Indian men in the princely States, etc.

Ques: Going on to ICU, can you talk about the kind of work you did there ?

Ans: At ICU, the nice thing was that they asked us what we'd like to do. I said I wanted to look at rural development schemes and compare them. In those days there were four or five major forms in which rural development was put on the ground. There was Khadi Village Industries Intensive Area Scheme. Then there was the famous S.K. Dey programme called the Community Development Projects—really well-organised packages; then they had the modified CDS, called the National Extension Scheme (NES) which was extending the more intensive community development project into a few others; and then there was *gram daan* which was Vinoba Bhave's way.

I asked ICU if I could do a study comparing and contrasting these four to see which was most effective. They agreed so I got on to that. We had Raj Krishna as our guide and if I said I wanted to see the intensive area he would say go to Bihar. Then I went off and walked with Vinoba and he introduced me to Annasaheb Sahasrabuddhe who was the country's leading constructive worker. Sahasrabuddhe asked me to go to Andhra Pradesh and Koraput in Orissa, so I travelled to all those villages and I did a monograph entitled *Evaluation of Rural Development.* Unfortunately, ICU lost the text. It was the most amazing baseline and I tell Lakshmi (Jain) that if it was published today I could get a Ph.D!

I was 23-24 years old then and footloose. I went and stayed with Achyut Patwardhan in Varanasi in his *ashram*. He made breakfast for me and took me to the Ganga. I looked at the intensive area projects in the Varanasi area, thanks to him. Then I lived in Koraput for 10 days in a *gram daan* village. So there were all these experiences and those days there were no computers so I typed it all and there was probably one carbon copy which also I left with them at ICU and went off to Harvard in 1958 for a 2-month seminar.

When I came back the ICU rural development division had been shifted and we just never found the document.

We used to have a lovely office in Yusuf Sarai on the way to the Qutub Minar, which was then a bus to rural India. We worked from this little house there in the villages in which we were given tables and chairs. Every Saturday morning, Lakshmi Jain, who was the general secretary of ICU, would have a conference retrieving what we had done and talking to each one of us. That's how we learnt what the other divisions of ICU were doing. We were the Research Division and then there was the Rural Credit Division and the Cottage Industries Division. It was very interesting and a tremendous education.

Ques: How long did you stay with ICU ?

Ans: I was with ICU for only a year and a half. After that I went to join Gunnar Myrdal as a research assistant for his book called *Asian Drama*. The reason I jumped at this was not because I did not like ICU. There was this Harvard International-Seminar that Kissinger used to organise—Lakshmi Jain had been chosen in 1954 and when he met me I think he and the others at ICU felt that I had the right potential to apply for that seminar. So they asked me to apply, which I did and I was selected.

So off I went at the age of 25 to America to attend this summer international seminar. Before I went, I heard from a friend that Myrdal was looking for a young economist assistant, so I went and met him. He agreed to take me and as it was a fantastic opportunity, I asked ICU to let me resign. Then I went to America for two months and I got a fellowship in America to travel through Asia. I told Myrdal if I was going to America, why not go through all the Asian countries about which he was writing. He felt it was a very good idea. I said I would raise my money for it. I was very lucky, because when I told Henry Kissinger (who was then a professor at Harvard) he said he would try and get me a scholarship from the Asia Foundation to pay for my halts and the extra for my tickets. He arranged that. So I went to every country, from Hawaii to Japan, to Vietnam, to Kampuchea, to Thailand. I even went to Burma which was closed at that time. All on my own, with no *per diem*. It was really amazing that one could do that without any STD phone calls, telegrams, faxes.

After America, I joined Myrdal and then my life moved away from ICU. After Myrdal, I went to Oxford, did Economics, came back to Delhi and taught at Miranda House for five years, then at Delhi School of Economics for one year. Then I resigned and started writing a book *Indian Women*, after which I got back to work by developing the Institute of Social Studies Trust (ISST)—which was the successor of the Research Division of ICU—which I did for fifteen years. My interest in women's issues came around 1974-75 when I wrote *Indian Women*. That book turned me. I went to Mexico for the women's conference and I got deeply into it.

Ques: Getting back to ICU, can you recall something about the atmosphere there during the time you were working with the organisation ?

Ans: The research department specifically was a very unstructured, unsupervised space. We had no full-time supervisor. Raj Krishna was teaching at Delhi College and he would come in a jeep in the morning after teaching, do his own work, in terms of his own writing (works published by ICU) and if we had any problem we would go to him. The atmosphere was one of tremendously put-on-your-own. We were all on our own. I remember this colleague, Kanta Nangia, who was once doing some work on milk cooperatives and who sometimes cried because there was no one to interact with. We were always told at our Saturday meetings: "Look, you should be on your own feet. Why should we find out where you can get information?" And in a way this was a challenge to all of us.

I would make my own programme. We would all be there on time in the mornings by 9.15 a.m but nobody would come and ask: when did you come, did you write your attendance, etc. It was a very free atmosphere and you were very much on your own. Most of us were just struggling away at the desk with our work. Individually, we were all extremely serious people. Whether this seriousness was an atmosphere of the time or not I can't say. But I must say this—and I myself am surprised—since I did ISST afterwards, I saw people who came for a job but didn't really work; people who came for a job but were always lamenting, complaining. At the research division in ICU we had nothing at all except tables and chairs and yet we were all glued to our work, often going home at 6 or 7 p.m.

ICU itself was a bit separated from us at the research division because its main activity seemed to be the Cottage Industries Emporium—that was its big beacon. I remember, at the research department we always felt somehow that we were creatures from outer space. Because those men and women at the Cottage were so vibrant, so all over the place. To a person like me who had come from the South, wore a saree and had long hair in a *jooda*, they all looked like fashion models, with matching *bindis* and all! To us they looked like very arty people. I'm sure they must have seen us as really crummy people. So we never had any interaction with the staff of the Cottage. The only interaction was with Lakshmi and Som Benegal, who was in charge of publications and Raj Krishna, who was our research adviser.

Gradually, however, I moved on from becoming a typical research employee to becoming a friend of Lakshmi, Som and others and then of course I fell in love with Lakshmi and that changed the relationship and I got to know all the beautiful Cottage Industries women very well!

Ques: Did you find your work at the research division challenging enough or did you find yourself getting restless ?

Ans: If I hadn't got the Kissinger and Myrdal offer, I would not only have stayed on at ICU but I would probably have had to build it up too. When I look back, from among the six researchers, perhaps intellectually and in terms of social leadership as well, I was the strongest. But I didn't stay long enough to show it.

I remember I had once written to Lakshmi about how he ought to reorganise ICU and he had written back saying : "You are really an intellectual and academic but you also tend to want to organise and you must make up your mind where you want to be. If you want to be an organiser then I can give you an organiser's job at ICU but if you want to do research then stay with it and don't try to tell us how to organise."

So I had got so deeply involved and there was no question of not being challenged. It was an exciting, wonderful place. You only had to enter that little area of Janpath to feel that something sensational was happening there.

I got to know Kamaladevi more and more. She was a distant figure but someone that one felt immediate respect for.

Ques: What was so special about the organisation ?

Ans: There was something innovative, aesthetically pleasant, ideologically meaningful happening at ICU and the most interesting part of it was Lakshmi. Lakshmi, when he conducted those meetings, was an exemplar. We were all young people but he was so inspiring that those meetings became one of the most lovely things you could ever attend because there was no domination, no management of learning, nor was there any *upadesham* like they do in the *ashrams*. But it was scintillating, inspiring and helpful.

I think it was those meetings that made all of us grow and made all of us recognise Lakshmi as a hidden power—a very muted, a very undominating but a very exciting person. He was very caring of everyone—he converted a leaf into a flower—and yet he managed to make us all perform well. This quality of his nature did make ICU a very nice place. But also people like Gopi Krishna, Kitty Shiva Rao—these were also very important people. Gopi Krishna who was in charge of rural cooperatives, was a very gentle, kind person who had a lot of respect for young researchers. Kitty Shiva Rao, whom I got to know more, was another person who had no hierarchy at all, although she was right on top as the Vice President. So they were exactly like a family. People were of that kind at that time, that era and you rarely see people like them these days. They took time off for you.

Ques: So was the excitement unique to those times or was ICU special in that sense ?

Ans: Let me speak for myself. I do think there was something about the time. I've written about this elsewhere too, that India was really open, interesting, it had no chips on its shoulder at all. It was self-confident—remember, we never had any problems like you now have of security, etc. Nehru would be in the AIFACS (All India Fine Arts and Crafts Society) watching a play with us and we'd all walk out together and we'd look at him as Panditji. There was no

SPG. Everything was so open. You'd find Americans, Canadians sitting and working with Indian NGOs like in ICU and you wouldn't feel they were CIA agents or that there was some patron-client relationship; the kind of heckles that we pick up now.

There was self-confidence among the Indians and the perception of Indians among Indians was that we were free, strong people. Today I think we Indians perceive ourselves as easily bought or sold. We are also petty now; we were not petty then.

I think ICU was partly a creature of the time and it was partly unique because it was reconstructing India, and it was teaching people from Nehru downwards that you can reconstruct with the people. I think, therefore, many of us who were engaged with it had the special excitement of ICU. But I think the environment was also very congenial.

Now I say this with some modesty. I don't know if my perception of that period was because I was 23-24 and today a 23-24-year-old woman might see all of India as very exciting. So I want to qualify my perceptions as being located at an age and a space.

Ques: What do you think went wrong with this very special organisation ?

Ans: Well, I lost track of the internal evolution of ICU partly because I went off with Myrdal in 1958 and I didn't come back till 1962. So I missed the critical time for ICU. Therefore, I'm not able to analyse it with knowledge.

But I do know that Kamaladevi and Lakshmi and Gopiji always had this ideology—which in a sense is partly Gandhian and partly the ideology of real freedom fighters—that no institution is worth its name if it has to be led by the same people. Any institution which persists in doing a job forever shows that the job is not well done. This whole concept of self-determination was so deeply embedded in Kamaladevi, Lakshmi, Gopiji and others that they didn't seem to have any attachment to what they had build up.

Speaking about myself, without intending it, I have also come out in the same way. When I was 58-59 and I had already built up ISST for 14 years from a file and a little stock of books and furnitures it inherited from ICU's Research Division to an organisation with capital worth a crore, 35 staff, well-established in the world and in India, I began to feel that this won't sustain itself unless I leave it now. I felt I had to prove to myself that I'd built up an institution and not a fiefdom. I had to prove to myself that there was an institution which had a life that I had breathed into it, but whose breath didn't depend upon me. At that time I hadn't remembered that this was Lakshmi's or Kamaladevi's ideology—I was doing it on my own fire. But now, over the last year or two when people have been quizzing me, I find I am forced to think about it and I feel maybe it is the same ethic that they had which is why they shed ICU.

They felt that if it was surviving it should be doing so for reasons other than the builders. In my opinion, ICU collapsed. There is no ICU. Lakshmi may say that ICU played its role and it was time to move on—that's one way of looking at the situation. But then the cooperative movement has come back and Lakshmi is now deeply into it. But Lakshmi does not believe that institutions should have a life, except people's institutions. I don't fully agree with this.

Ques: Would you say as some of the others do, that one of the reasons for this collapse was that ICU was too idealistic ?

Ans: No, not at all. I think institutions like ICU and ISST should exist only if they're idealistic and visionary. I am simply against NGOs trying to be pragmatic, if their aim is the removal of inequality and poverty. I think institutions like ICU were born only for that —not to become institutions for the sake of institutions, but for addressing poverty and inequality. They were also there to show that people had the strength to build their own lives. These are the three pillars that set the idealistic basic principles. Many people feel that if ICU had been more realistic it would have survived. Why should it survive? When survival becomes a basic principle, then those visions go.

In my view, all NGOs—if they want to belong to the voluntary sector, which is what they claim—have no business to be in the game unless they have an idealistic vision; a vision, which surpasses normal human frailty. This is where I think there is a loss among the NGOs all over the world. Those NGOs which are born out of an ideological chord like Marxism, or Gandhism, or the Progressive Jesuits, they at least have the feeling that they are there as a means to an end; that they are facilitators towards an end, which is justice. All other NGOs are parasites who are becoming development agents, cloning themselves on the government and private sector, saying they are practical and pragmatic. I'm very clear in my mind that it is only vision and that totally revolutionary role that makes an NGO, otherwise they should wither away. That's why I'm partially with Lakshmi who feels that institution building for its own sake makes you trade off that dazzling revolutionary edge; it distracts you from the vision and the mission.

And this is exactly what happened to Cottage Industries. From being an organisation that was born to help artisans, it has become an organisation that is there to help the sales people. It has totally changed. Today, if you go to the sales people there, I don't think they even know who are the people who got them there. They are just like any other shop.

Ques: Why and how did the research division at ICU come to a close ?

Ans: It happened gradually. Because the researchers basically moved out, and they moved out because I think there was not much spurring happening. And ICU itself was also moving like this. The whole rural credit programme was misunderstood, and the ideological stance that Nehru and others took regarding collective farming made ICU the scapegoat as if they were selling American cooperatives rather than selling Gandhi's cooperatives. I was not there at that time but by the time I came back, there was no research division. However, in one sense I kept my links with ICU since ISST was given birth to by ICU.

Ques: Looking back over the entire ICU experience, what would you say ICU gave to you ?

Ans: It did a lot. For example, it was from ICU that I learnt what it is to belong to an institution. It was my first experience with an

NGO and that determined my life and afterwards I was able to build an NGO like ISST which I couldn't have done without ICU.

Secondly, it has not been recorded, but I was responsible for the birth of AVARD (Association of Voluntary Agencies in Rural Development). After I did this comparative study of rural development, I came back very excited, feeling that all these agencies needed to be networked and that we should have an association of these agencies. So everyone said what should we do and I said let's found an organisation. So they asked me to write it, which I did, and I called it AVARD. I actually sat and worked on it and at that time Sitaram Goel was also asked to look after it. He then drew up the constitution and some others also joined in.

And of course, I would never have known the idealism of post-Independence India (because I was too young), if it had not been for the ICU spirit. Then, there was my interaction with Kamaladevi and later on as Lakshmi's friend and then as his wife, and meeting his associates like Rajkrishna, Gopiji the Benegals, Una, Teji Vir Singh and others, all very beautiful and fine people who determined my life in so many ways. So the ICU experience for me was a very strong factor in my life after 1958 and particularly in my life after 1964.

❑ ❑ ❑

EIGHTEEN

"Cooperatives should not only give out loans and credits but they should become an integral part of the entire social awakening process."

— *Amba Prasad*

Ques: How far back does your association with the cooperative movement go ?

Ans: From 1942-44, during the Independence struggle, I was in jail for three years. I had finished only my matriculation then. It was during those three years in jail that I got interested in education and realised that I am nothing without education. So in 1945, after release from jail, I came to Delhi and joined Hindu College. My family was opposed to my involvement in politics—they were feudal lords. I knew nobody here. In the mornings I would go to college and in the evenings I would do trade union work and give tuitions.

In 1946, I got involved in the student movement. It was here that I came in touch with Lakshmi Jain and got active in the student movement. Lakshmi and I were together in the student Congress; he was the President of the Delhi Student Congress and I was the Secretary. So we worked together during our college days and in the freedom movement around 1946-47. Then Lakshmi went on to the Faridabad project and I went on to the Delhi Pradesh Congress Committee where I was the office secretary.

In those days the cooperative movement was taken as a movement for the poor. Even before I formally joined the Delhi State Cooperative Union, I had started three cooperatives in the Pradesh Congress Committee. I began a cooperative for cycle-rickshaw pullers. We were the first to break the monopoly on cycle-rickshaws by politicians The second cooperative I started was for dead animal lifters. A factory was set up and every part of the dead animal was utilised. Then I also sent those people to Khadi Gram Udyog in Bombay, for training in utilisation of carcasses. The third cooperative society was a transport society—taxis and tempos. All the three were working very well till there was a split in the Congress

Committee and then within three years, everything closed down due to political interference.

In 1958, the Congress was divided and Subhadra Joshi dismissed me from the Pradesh Congress Committee. This was when I went to Lakshmi and said to him: "I am unemployed; I have absolutely nothing. From tomorrow onwards, how am I going to live?" He promptly handed me the register of an institution—it was called the Delhi Cooperative Institute, which he and some others had registered a long time back.

He gave me this register and a ten-rupee note saying: "Here you are, now you develop this Cooperative Institute." This was an institute meant for developing the cooperative movement in Delhi; for educating the people; educating members of cooperatives and also for training employees of cooperative societies.

I was to develop this Institute and my salary of Rs. 300 a month would be reimbursed by the Indian Cooperative Union. So that was also the beginning of my connection with ICU. It was the job of ICU to develop the cooperative movement and encourage its members. Although this institute had been registered, it had been lying dormant for three years, till I was given the responsibility of developing it.

Late Brahm Perkash provided the space in Daryaganj and Lakshmi gave me the moral and technical support. And this is how it began. Later—after about five years—it was converted into the Delhi State Cooperative Union, according to the policy of the Government of India, because in all the States we have state cooperative unions. I became its secretary, Lakshmi was general secretary and Brahm Parkash was the president. Our office was in the Delhi State Cooperative Bank and from there we started our training programme, effectively developing cooperatives in Delhi.

Ques: Can you elaborate on this training programme ?

Ans: Well, since a centrally sponsored scheme had been initiated at the same time, we took the assistance of the Delhi Administration and we set up a separate training centre for the training of regular employees of cooperative societies. A separate institute at Kamla Nagar was set up under the auspices of the Delhi Cooperative Union. Members' education was continued with the instructors to train the general members of cooperative societies.

Ques: What was the scope and significance of this training ?

Ans: It included help in auditing, instruction in holding regular elections, talks on the powers of the managing committee, the Cooperative Societies Act and Rules, how to obtain government assistance, how to create more cooperatives, and other such facets of the cooperative movement. This was the main programme and it continued for a long time, almost till around 1969. Moreover, this was the sole institute in Delhi to conduct such a programme. Lakshmi was its general secretary and he provided all the support and guidance for this.

For the first five years, both the financial and technical support was given to us by ICU. B.L. Dhar came regularly to our training programmes and, in fact, he addressed the first training programme that we held. One of the most important aspects of the institute was that all the planning for development of cooperatives—whether they were State cooperatives, or the federation for fertilisers and seeds, etc.—was prepared by us. I must say that the contribution of ICU in this was great.

During this period in 1961, Lakshmi felt that I should go for some training myself. He sent me for two months' training at the National Centre for Cooperative Education in Gurgaon. Later, I was to become the Principal of the same Centre which had then shifted to Delhi.

Again in 1963, Lakshmi sponsored me for a two-month UNESCO scholarship for training in cooperatives in Japan. This was a very significant event in my life—seeing the honesty and dedication of the Japanese people, changed my entire outlook. Japan was the most developed country as far as multipurpose cooperatives were concerned. This was a very useful experience for me particularly in the area of farmers' cooperatives, since we had similar cooperatives because Jawaharlal Nehru had put a lot of emphasis on that. It was a fascinating experience—not just seeing the working of the cooperatives but also observing the personal character of the Japanese people—there was a lot to learn in terms of their work ethics. Even as far as the cooperatives were concerned, it was interesting to see the multifarious activities that they had taken up—cooperatives in Japan were organising even social events like weddings and funerals.

So this was a totally new concept for me, that cooperatives should not only be giving out loans and credit, but that they should become an integral part of the entire social awakening process.

Ques: How long did the training programme go on ?

Ans: In 1969, the Congress was defeated and the Jana Sangh came to power which cancelled the grant of the state cooperative union. So, in 1969, I was again unemployed and this time Brahm Parkash offered me a job as Principal of the National Centre for Cooperative Education in the National Cooperative Union of India. Therefore, I became an employee of the National Cooperative Union and continued as secretary of the Delhi State Cooperative Union.

Ques: But at some stage before this you were also actively involved with the Super Bazar. Can you recall your experiences there ?

Ans: In July, 1966, when Indira Gandhi asked Lakshmi to set up the Super Bazar, he and N.N. Dutta called me. From the very first day I was given charge of market intelligence and member relations. Lakshmi wanted to ensure that whatever we were selling was competitive and was priced lower than in the market. It was very interesting and challenging work.

I continued for 16 years in the Super Bazar. I was a paid employee of the National Cooperative Union of India; I was an honorary consultant for training and market intelligence in the Super Bazar.

At the training institute where I worked, there was a Swedish cooperator, Herman Lamn, who was training in-charge of consumer cooperatives. He and I initiated a training programme in the Super Bazar. The training was divided into two parts: one for the employees and the other for the members.

For my market intelligence, I was given a small sum which I had to use to make actual purchases from the market. For instance, if there was a particular item we were selling for Rs. 20 a kg, then I had to find out its rate in Khari Baoli, in INA, in Patel Nagar, etc. Our man would go there, actually make the purchases and see the price and quality. That is the work I did for 16 years, until politics again intervened.

Ques: Then what went wrong ?

Ans: Well, Sanjay Gandhi appointed Arjun Das as Vice President and it all began going wrong. To give one example: They were buying coolers from Kamla Market at Rs. 750 a piece. On the Super Bazar invoices it was marked at Rs. 1,100 and they sold it for Rs. 1,200 or so, while Kamla Market sold exactly the same cooler for Rs. 800. Arjun Das did not like my pointing this out, having a vested interest in the purchases for the Super Bazar.

Ques: Was any action taken on things like this ?

Ans: I did a detailed report saying that there was something terribly wrong with all this. Arjun Das flared up. He said to me: "We are supplying to the government, why should you bother about the consumer?" I told him it was immaterial whether we were selling to the government or to anyone else; that the issue here was one of the Super Bazar's integrity and honesty in dealing with the consumer. I insisted that I would publish this report and send it to the general manager, Dharm Dutt, who, unfortunately, was a very weak and timid fellow and he didn't do anything about it. So I resigned.

I had retired from the National Cooperative Union of India and joined the Lok Kalyan Samiti (LKS) of which I was the founder member, since 1954. Though in LKS my job was different I did not lose my interest in cooperatives.

I had been feeling badly about the Super Bazar for a long time. The presidents were very weak persons. It had become completely politicised and had lost its true character of serving the consumer. The posts of chairman, one after the other, were all political appointments. After L.C. Jain, there was not a single case of the president of the Super Bazar being a cooperator. And since the capital was given by the government, the general manager was a bureaucrat. Anyone who did not desire to go out of Delhi manipulated deputations to the Super Bazar. Thus, the Bazar became a resting place for IAS officers. It became a very frustrating situation.

I had also started a Hindi magazine for consumers, entitled *Super Bazar Patrika*. It was a beautiful, 24-page monthly magazine for creating consumer consciousness. Some pages were devoted to comparative prices. After I left, it was reduced to four pages and it went on like that. However, the systems we had introduced continued, and are giving good results.

But let us not forget that we also had people like Roop Narain who was in charge of the purchase of groceries. He was given Rs. 4 crores annually for purchases and not a single sample of Surf powder or anything ever went to his house, so honest and dedicated was he. You see, Lakshmi had a knack of selecting the right people for the right jobs. People like Roop Narain, like N.N. Datta, the general manager, B.L. Dhar, etc.

But today you know what is happening there in the purchases.

Ques: Why were things allowed to deteriorate in this manner ?

Ans: It happened with the appointment of an IAS officer as the general manager instead of getting someone from the cooperative movement, genuinely interested in consumer protection. After N.N. Datta left, there was no such person there. So all the people who had come to the Super Bazar from the Cottage Industries Emporium gradually began to leave.

The Super Bazar was started within 15 days' time—everyone was on the job. Later, N.N. Datta managed beautifully well and we started a regular training programme for the employees. But when the politicians came, they started recruiting the area's musclemen who wore gold chains and were unable to speak any language properly. So you see, the entire cooperative movement was defaced by these politicians and the bureaucracy.

There was one bureaucrat, J.N. Gupta, who had some dedication. He tried to put the balance-sheet in order. He gave us complete respect. I remember, I once sent him a report on a handloom item that we purchased from Chandni Chowk but was being sold at double the price at the Super Bazar. He immediately took action and sacked that handloom purchase officer. But J.N. Gupta who was there for about 3-4 years was an exception. By and large, the most inefficient men were sent to the Super Bazar. This is not to say that the entire IAS cadre is bad, but nobody really wanted to come to the Super Bazar—only those people came here who did not want a posting somewhere else.

In our days the Super Bazar was a pace-setter in many ways—in its packaged commodities, its self-service system, prices being marked on the packets. In fact, you got everything from a coffee shop to a hair dressing saloon, to groceries, under one roof. All said and done, the Super Bazar was a fascinating place and I enjoyed working there; just as I also enjoyed the teaching and training. And that was the reason why even after people like Datta and Lakshmi had gone, I continued.

Now nobody works for the employees, nobody works for training, nobody is in consumer protection. And this, when consumer courts have come up, consumer protection is being talked about. We were the first people in Delhi to start the consumer movement; Super Bazar was the first to start the consumer protection movement and we should take credit for it. Every month we would have the members' meeting and they were involved. Now they don't want any member's participation, they don't want employees' participation —there's nothing. They don't even want to work for profit, because if you work for profit then you have to sell; if you have to sell then you have to be competitive; if you have to be competitive, then you have to improve your standard—this will lead you to efficient working because you can't make profit without efficiency. But now they're not worried about profit; they're not worried about anything.

Ques: What is your opinion of cooperatives today ?

Ans: My own interest in cooperatives continues. But I feel that today cooperatives are completely out of tune in the country. Now you don't expect anything from them. Under globalisation and privatisation schemes, there has arisen a question mark about the very place and relevance of Corporatives. But having said all this, I still feel that if you want real people's participation, there is no other institution except cooperatives which can bring people together.

❑ ❑ ❑

INDEX